MW00343604

The Savvy Samoyed

Pat Hill Goodrich

*Best wishes to Suzanne
— Pat Hill Goodrich*

Copyright © 2001 by Pat Hill Goodrich

All rights reserved. No part of this publication may be reproduced or transmitted in any form or by any means, electronically or mechanically, including photocopying, recording, or by any information storage or retrieval system, without the prior written permission of the publisher.

Published by Doral Publishing, Sun City, Arizona
Printed in the United States of America.

Copyedited by MaryEllen Smith
Interior Design by The Printed Page
Cover by Masterpiece Publishing

Library of Congress Card Number: 2001091729
ISBN: 0-944875-70-X

Publisher's Cataloging-in-Publication
(*Provided by Quality Books, Inc.*)

Goodrich, Pat Hill.
   The savvy Samoyed / Pat Hill Goodrich. -- 1st ed.
   p. Cm. -- (The purebreds ; 12)
   Includes bibliographical references and index.
   LCCN: 2001091729
   ISBN: 0-944875-70-X

   1. Samoyed dog.   I. Title.

SF429.S35G66 2001   636.73
             QBI01-201018

In memory of

Fanya Felice and Rocky

Acknowledgments

For their inspiration and information, along with steadfast encouragement, I am grateful to my dear husband, Bill, who is my in-house editor and cheering section; Flo and Saul Waldman; Marion Langlois; untiring researcher Billie Danz; Diane Sorrentino; Dr. Jody Guinn; Don and Dot Hodges; Sandra Olsen; Heather Schmidt; Susan Amundsen; Sue Waldman; Dr. David Quick; Wilna Coulter; Sally Paulissen; Amelia Price; Carol Brown; Judges Bunny Hyman, Frank Grover, and Catherine Bell; Joan Froling; Pat deBack; Sandra Flettner; Sharon Parker; Alice Thompson Lombardi; Brian Amm, R.C.M.P.; Dr. A. L. Reed; Dr. U. V. Mostosky; Jerry Wolfe; George Alston; Sandra Davis; Kathy Kennedy; Lisa Peterson; Lynn Godbee; Louis Thompson; Scott Vail; Dr. Gary G. Keller; Sheila Herrmann; Dr. Larry Glickman; Dr. M. K. Herrmann; Susan Mitterling; Diana Garcia; Dr. E. .A. Corley; Dr. J. B. Kaneene; Becky Bunnell; Betsy Anderson; Vi O'Neill of 4M Books; and the staff of the U. S. Army Military History Institute.

Special commendation goes to Joyce Cutler, who has gone beyond the call of friendship to do the final typing for me.

A special thank you to Dr. Alvin Grossman and Lynn Grey of Doral Publishing Inc. for their interest and encouragement in this endeavor, as well as MaryEllen Smith, my editor, for her expertise and enthusiasm.

My apologies go to any others who may be left off this list. Once I can shovel off my desk and its environs, more could come to light. I am grateful to all of you for your many kindnesses.

Note from the Author

I do not claim to know all the answers, but have had Samoyeds as family members since 1969; they have taught me most of what I do know. They also devise daily the next installment of my continuing education course.

A portion of the proceeds from this book will be donated to the Texas chapter of the Samoyed Rescue Organization.

A two-year-old Franklin Delano Roosevelt (1884) and his dog "Buddy" sit atop a donkey. Buddy, who may have been a Samoyed, was given to the Roosevelt family by a member of a European royal house.

Courtesy of FDR Museum, Hyde Park, New York

*"The Samoyed is an intelligent dog,
and very few people **in the world** can handle that!"*

—George Alston
Professional handler extraordinaire,
teacher, speaker, and author

Contents

Introduction

"If dogs are all about love, then Samoyeds are the dogs that love beyond the expectation of what we truly deserve.

"Yes, you will tell new owners that the puppy should not be allowed on the couch or bed. Yet you know in your heart that the sofa will be his throne. Without a peep from the owner, the muddy footprints will track across the white ceramic tiles to where the Sammy lies sleeping. The house will be redecorated in the appropriate colors—beiges, whites, and muted shades—that reveal little evidence of the shedding.

"A smiling face. A buddy when the world doesn't understand. A dog who can live anywhere, adapt to your lifestyle, and do virtually any activity. Other dog owners may believe that only their species is love and happiness all wrapped up in one, but if you have ever owned a Samoyed, you know better."

—*Amelia Price of Bubbling Oaks Samoyeds*

Hundreds of years ago, in the snowy and treeless vastnesses of Siberia, the lives of the Samoyede people depended upon their magnificent white dogs. These creatures were needed to keep them warm, tow their belongings on icy trails as they moved about, drive herds of wild reindeer to their camp, and chase off marauding packs of wolves. As if these chores were not enough, the dogs also hunted the polar bear, the insatiably ravenous scourge of the North.

Transported to climes where he has had to learn the proper use of a tree, the modern Samoyed finds himself in charge of a family no longer in dire need of a forager, a herder, a transporter, or a warm furry sleeping companion. At times, his ancestors seem to stir in his soul, calling to him in dreams of nebulous visions of white sweeping Arctic vistas.

Because of the conflict between his modern surroundings and the call of the wild in his soul, this poor fellow can be at a loss for something to do. As a working dog, he requires assignments. If given none, his intelligent and active mind will likely invent his own entertainment, some of which will undoubtedly cause you displeasure.

Ch. Czar Nicholas Lebanov at the piano on board the ship "Delta Queen" on the way to Sacramento from San Francisco, taken in 1939. The seated choir: Dascha, Varka, Petrof, Katinka

Breed uniformity adherence to the standard. Remington and Thompson of the Seven Samurai (litter of all boys)

Some Sams will adopt a toy, a chew bone, or even a local kitten to carry and cherish all day. When the novelty wears off, he may call to other dogs to liven things up. "Look what I got! Come get it if you can!" If alone and bored, he may decide to soar over fences, charge through the neighborhood, and head for the wide-open spaces in search of amusement.

A Samoyed's first priority is to care for his human family. He will, however, also enjoy agility classes, relay races, and therapy visits to hospitals. Occasional tracking exercises or herding trials gladden his heart with the requirement to chase something. Scarcely believing his good fortune, he can be counted on to participate with gusto.

In the show ring, the Samoyed heads happily to his destination, his fluffy beauty eliciting gasps of admiration on the way. With his spectacular coat and angelic expression, he seems to be the misfit of the working group. He may be sabotaged by his dazzling looks. Perhaps he should wear a sign around his neck saying, "I hunted polar bears, for pete's sake! Has anybody else here done that?" This dog is not just another pretty face.

Because the Samoyed is so unique and engages its owner on so many levels, I wish to stress that this book can serve as an alternative to owning one. This breed is not for everyone. If you do not have the time to house, tend, train, socialize, understand, and be a close companion for a Sam, please do not acquire one. I pray that nothing will be done to encourage puppy mills that ruin the breed and cause the dogs irreparable misery and distress.

There are many alternatives to ownership. You can enjoy reading about the breed; you can do volunteer work for a Samoyed rescue organization; or, perhaps, try to locate an owner who will allow you to get acquainted with his Sam. You could visit them now and then, or even Sammy-sit sometimes.

Other canine-related activities include urging local and regional groups of legislators to ban puppy mills; organizing groups to educate the public, and especially school children, about the proper care and treatment of animals; and collecting funds that will purchase bullet-proof vests for police dogs. Surprisingly, many law enforcement departments have low to no funds for this important K-9 protection.

On a larger scale, you may choose to do as Houstonian Heather Schmidt has done: she founded The Samoyed Rescue of Southwest Texas, as well as a chapter of Noah's Ark Animal Sanctuary. The latter accepts from shelters animals about to be euthanized because no one wants them. Heather rescues them and finds them good homes, too.

Although you may not have a Sam of your own, you can help all animals by doing good deeds for all these loving creatures who need help.

Chapter 1

The Samoyede People and Their Origins

By William A Goodrich, M. D.

The peoples bearing the Samoyede name have, for centuries, lived in the tundra and forests of northern Russia and Siberia, in the region of the Arctic Circle. This domain is generally considered to reach from 40 to 100 degrees longitude (but predominantly in the region from 60 to 80 degrees longitude), and north of the 57th degree of latitude.[1] This area encompasses the Kanin, Yamal, and Taymyr peninsulas, and the lands around the Ob, Pur, Taz, Yenesey, and Pechora rivers. It includes the tundra both east and west of the upper extent of the Ural mountains.

Interestingly, the exact origin of the name of "Samoyede" is unclear. It is not used by the indigenous peoples, and is not a part of the Russian language. Presumably it is of Russian origin, dating back to the intermittent Czarist conquests in the thirteenth and sixteenth centuries. The Russian name "Yurak," used to designate specific Nenets people, is not used by the natives, either. It is pronounced "Sam-(a)-yed," the "yed" almost "yet," with stress on third syllable, and not "Sammy-Ed." The latter may have mistakenly evolved from the

Dale Evans and Roy Rogers admire three
Mason Samoyeds exhibited by Lloyd Van Sickle
at a sportsman's show in Los Angeles

Courtesy of Sandra Flettner

vernacular nicknames "Sams" or Sammies." According to a Finnish researcher, "oy" is not pronounced in the middle of the word "Samoyed."

The third syllable is accented and the **o** is pronounced like the long **a**, according to Dr. Pierre Hart, long-time professor of Russian at Louisiana State University. He states that linguistically the word is related somewhat to the Finno-Ugric language group, which includes languages of the Finns, Estonians, Hungarians, and others.[2]

Five peoples are called Samoyedes: Nenets (or Urak Samoyedes), Enets, Nganasan, Sel'kup, and Kamas. The Soviet census in 1959 showed only a total of 30,000 persons for all five groups. Eighty-three percent are the Nenets. The languages of the five are similar but distinct, and there are similarities to Finnish, which suggests a common origin in Siberia with later separation and migration of these peoples to the north.[3]

Indeed, the life styles of the various Samoyedes and the Laplanders are comparable. They are nomadic, live in tents, and subsist largely on reindeer, which supply both food and hides for clothing and tents. This existence is quite like that of the plains Indians of North America, except that their buffalo were not domesticated, the American plains are less frigid, and the Arctic dog is used by the Samoyedes for herding and sledding.

The Samoyedes often use reindeer as well as Samoyed dogs to pull sleds. The Nenets use their dogs more for herding, however, which allows a few men to oversee hundreds or thousands of animals.[4]

In contrast, in recent times the Sel'kup Samoyedes use dogs more for sledding than herding. It is known that this group tends to let their reindeer run wild, rounding them up periodically and/or hunting them as one would undomesticated animals.

Ch. Starshine's Adoraduk O'Fanya in her Porsche—ready to go!

Photo by Pat Goodrich

Ch. Sno Dawn's Guipago O'Kazakh

*Courtesy of Diane Sorrentino,
Owner/Breeder, Sno Dawn
Samoyeds*

The Arctic herding dog is apparently also called "layka." It is thought the dog was more widely used in primitive times, before reindeer domestication.

Some modern Nenets have accepted permanent settlements and agriculture, though many still prefer the migratory life as clearly demonstrated by a 1998 *National Geographic* article entitled *Nenets: Surviving on the Siberian Tundra.*[5] This split among the peoples allows the government and its administrators to oversee taxation and render judicial decisions with greater ease.

End Notes

1   *Encyclopedia Britannica* (Atlas), Vol. 24, (1936), pp. 48, 56, 57.

2   *Interview with Dr. Pierre Hart*, Professor of Russian, Louisiana State University, Baton Rouge.

3   Peter Hajdu, *The Samoyede Peoples and Languages* (Bloomington: Indiana University Press), 1963.

4   *Personal communication from Heather Schmidt* via the WWW, 1997.

5   Fen Montaigne, "Nenets: Surviving on the Siberian Tundra," *National Geographic*, Vol. 193, No. 3, March 1998.

The Doctor and the...Professor?

Bill (Dr. William Goodrich, author of this chapter) sat watching television with Pixie stretched across his lap, asleep on her back, paws neatly folded on her chest. "Would you hand me the remote, please?" he called to his wife. "She gets mad if I move."

Dr. Bill Goodrich and Remington partying (the latter in a tux—top hat nearby).

Chapter 2

From Polar Expeditions to England and America

Samoyed dogs were used on several Arctic expeditions during the late-eighteenth and early-nineteenth centuries. At least a measure of the success of these historic journeys that mapped unknown areas, recorded weather, and acquired scientific data has been attributed to the use of the breed. They enabled the explorers to navigate the vast, frozen lands and cope with the brutal conditions awaiting them.

Dr. Fridtjof Nansen, the Norwegian scientist, explorer, statesman, and Nobel Prize winner, was the first European explorer to use the Samoyed sledge dogs. In 1897, the journal from his 1893 Arctic expedition was published in two volumes entitled *Farthest North*. On this second of his many journeys north, Nansen had planned to let his ship, the *Fram* (the Norwegian word for forward), freeze in the ice of the Arctic ocean in order to establish the existence of a trans-Polar current. He hoped that the ship would drift westward with the ice. However, Nansen soon became restless and left the ship with part of his crew and the dog teams in order to explore the frozen land on foot. He and a crew member, Hjalmar Johansen, reached a point farther north than any man had yet attained. Eventually, both Nansen and the *Fram* returned safely from this trip, having proven the existence of

Fanya rides, Rocky pulls, Pixie plays…they love to keep busy.

Photo by Alvin Gee

both a deep Arctic ocean and a trans-Polar current (although the Pole itself was not reached on this expedition).

Although none of the dogs survived, Nansen was pleased with their performance and wrote admiringly of their intellect, loyalty, and courage in the environment of the frozen tundra.

In 1894, the Jackson-Harmsworth expedition to Franz Joseph Land took along Samoyed dogs on Nansen's recommendation. Captain Jackson described being saved by two of them after having been cornered by a polar bear. The dogs that survived this trip were sent to England. Nimrod, one of Jackson's Samoyeds and an especially marvelous bear hunter, was hit by a train after reaching civilization—a tragic ending for such a noble dog. His name does, however, appear in some early pedigrees.

An 1898 Italian expedition led by the Duc d'Abruzzi also followed Nansen's advice about using Samoyeds.

Another 1898 expedition, led by the Norwegian Carsten Borchgrevnik, traveled from New Zealand to the Antarctic. This British enterprise used Samoyeds that had been bought in Siberia. On returning to New Zealand, the dogs were left at Stewart Island.

In 1903, Captain Robert Scott aimed for the North Pole with Samoyeds acquired in Siberia. The dogs used by Borchgrevnik traveled north again on a 1907 expedition, along with some ponies that Sir Ernest Shackleton, another great Arctic explorer, preferred. Shackleton used only dogs on his later Arctic journeys.

Explorer Roald Amundsen reached the South Pole on December 14, 1911, and was the first to accomplish this feat. He took exceptional care of his teams of Samoyeds and Eskimo dogs.

In 1913, Dr. Nansen was invited to accompany a group of men who wished to open a regular trade route through Siberia. The traders thought that the land could provide nearly unlimited supplies of timber, grain, and other resources valuable to international commerce. Unfortunately, their Siberia Company had failed to reach the Yenesei the previous year. Their chartered Norwegian steamer was built to cope with ice, but the ship encountered such great quantities of it in that success was impossible. Nansen's experience with Arctic conditions in previous years and his thorough education made him an invaluable consultant.

Because others were managing the mechanics of the expedition, Dr. Nansen was free to observe the natives' manner of coping with the severe weather, as well as their customs.

Having seen the Samoyed dogs for the first time on his own Arctic explorations, Nansen paid particular attention to the beautiful, white-furred creatures. He recorded numerous curiosities, including some unusual uses for the dogs. In addition to their conventional winter chores of sledging, hunting, and herding, the Samoyeds also towed fishing boats along the banks of streams in the summer. The dogs appeared to enjoy their work, and they seemed happy to be allowed to ride in the boats when going downstream.

The native peoples often had broad, flat baking ovens, which provided warm sleeping places. Wives often claimed these spots. However, when a family's dogs returned from a trip, the weary canines got the privileged accommodations. The natives, he observed, were fond of their dogs and took good care of them.

"I...saw so many fine powerful sledge dogs," he wrote, adding that "all traffic during the long winter" was carried by reindeer and dogs, all of which made good speed.

Some of the Samoyeds prevented Jonas Lied, the manager of the Siberia Company, from keeping a promise to Nansen and the others regarding a dinner of wooly mammoth steaks. The dogs had dug up the frozen extinct beast and eaten most of it. Nansen wrote that he was relieved, for he had had recurring thoughts of contracting food poisoning from consuming something that had lain frozen deep in the earth for thousands of years. Incidentally, the dogs also dug up a wooly rhinoceros on one occasion.

Dr. Nansen said that he was puzzled at how these extinct animals lay practically intact, with bones, flesh, skin, and hair enclosed in the eternally frozen soil. He wondered how they could have frozen before putrefaction set in, and remain so well preserved that the dogs feasted on the beasts without ill effects. A fellow explorer stated that, on an expedition to the Lyckhov Islands, his dogs dug up the bones of extinct animals that had been frozen in slopes of sand to eat the marrow from them.

Nansen did not believe that there had been glaciers in that area. He felt it unlikely these animals could have been preserved in many different places by accident. He also noted that the huge creatures were embedded in frozen layers of sand or clay, not ice. This was a mystery that remains, perhaps, unsolved to this day.

The foundation of the present day Samoyed is said to be predicated on the dogs that survived these polar expeditions. It is important to know the history of these earliest dogs, whose names appear in the beginning pedigrees. Fortunately, some photographs and articles exist from English papers of the 1920s and 1930s that document the progress of the breed after it was transplanted from its native climes.

In 1889, the first Samoyed, named Sabarka, was given as a gift by Ernest Kilburn Scott to his wife. Soon they imported Whitey Pechora from Siberia for breeding purposes. Two of the puppies from these two dogs were Peter the Great and Neva.

Lady Sitwell imported a male, named Musti, from Siberia. She then bought Neva. Nansen, the sire of several champions, was the offspring

B'Dazzle raids the refrigerator. Being a house dog offers lots of opportunities for gourmet meals.

Photo by Pat Goodrich

of Musti and Whitey Pechora. Lady Sitwell also bred the first Samoyed champion, Olaf Oussa.

In 1894, a male named Russ was sent to the Kilburn Scotts. He was bred to Kvik and produced Pearlene, the second champion Samoyed and the first bitch champion. The third champion, Alaska, who was owned by Mrs. MacLaren Morrison, came from the breeding of Russ and Flo.

In 1899, Captain Frederick Jackson gave the Kilburn Scotts Nimrod, his bear dog, in addition to Kvik, Flo, Yugor, Mamax, and Gladys. It was said that the bitches Kvik and Flo had the finest influence on the breed. Jackson gave Alexandra, the British Queen, Flo's half brother, Jacko. She had several other Samoyeds in her kennels at Sandringham, and showed her dogs frequently.

The Kilburn Scotts acquired Antarctic Buck from the Sydney Zoo in 1908. A most important sire, he passed along his excellent conformation and glistening white coat to his progeny. Buck himself was descended from the dogs of the Borchgrevnik expedition.

Pixie plays the piano
Photo by Pat Goodrich

In 1892, under the influence of the Kilburn Scotts, the breed was officially named "Samoyede" after the people who had kept them for many centuries. Soon the second **e** was dropped.

In 1893 the dogs were first shown as a foreign breed. England's Kennel Club began registering them in 1901, and gave the Samoyed official recognition in 1909. That year also saw the establishment of the breed standard under the influence of early fanciers, including the Kilburn Scotts, who are credited with having the most influence in saving and establishing the breed. They began breeding for a consistent and recognized type in 1896. They decided to make the white coat the breed's benchmark (there was then no other medium-sized white show dog with a long coat), and exclude the brown, black, and spotted-coated dogs that were sometimes seen in Siberia. The majority of Samoyeds found there, however, were white. It is said that there was at least one black and white champion, but the colored dogs sometimes showed mongrel traits.

Another important event of 1909 was the organization of the first Samoyed breed club for men. Women soon formed their own organization. Later the two merged, creating the Samoyed Association of Great Britain. Frederick Jackson was the first president, holding the office until he died in 1938.

A Belgian countess, Princess de Montyglyon, introduced the breed to America when she immigrated there in 1904. She brought along her Samoyed, Moustan, who had been delivered to her railway coach in a basket of orchids and roses—a fitting backdrop for a Samoyed. The Grand Duke Michael, brother of Czar Nicholas II, had heard her admire the dog at a show in Russia. In 1906, Moustan became the first Samoyed to be registered by the American Kennel Club. His pedigree was unknown but he sired the first American champion, de Witte of Argentau.

The Samoyed Club of America (SCA) was founded in 1923. It based its constitution and breed standard on that of the English club. Three months later, the SCA was approved for membership by the American Kennel Club (AKC). Its first president was Mr. Louis Smirnow. Samoyeds were first placed in the Non-Sporting Group in England, then in the Herding Group in the United States. Later, when the versatility of the breed was more fully recognized, Samoyeds were placed in the Working Group, where they remain today.

In her book, *Your Samoyed*, Jan Kauzlarich documents the early history of the Samoyed, as well as that of founding kennels in Great Britain and the United States. Other informative books used in writing this chapter were *The Samoyed* by the Samoyed Association of Great Britain, *Samoyeds* by W. Lavallin Puxley, and *This Is the Samoyed* by Joan McDonald Brearley. The information provided by these books is important to owners and breeders alike. It is interesting to know that the modern Samoyed descended from such illustrious forebears.

Another Siberian Journey

Mr. Smirnoff of Smirnoff Vodka, a very elderly man, told one of the California kennel clubs how much he loved Samoyeds. He said that when he and his family were escaping from the Bolsheviks in Russia, a team of Samoyeds transported them to safety across the Siberian wastelands. They continued on through Alaska and Canada to the mainland U.S., where he founded the eponymous vodka company.

Chapter 3

A Most Versatile Working Dog

The blood that surges through the veins of the beautiful, sensitive Samoyed compels them to hearken back to their ancestors, who belonged, for hundreds of years, to the relatively small group of Samoyede people in Siberia.

These days, Sams must still live closely with their families, or they will become intensely unhappy and will not fully develop their capabilities as intuitive partners to their human associates. Knowing something of their heritage is critical in understanding and appreciating this reputedly purest breed.

In Siberia, Samoyeds were considered equal members of the family—partners in the daily ordeal of survival in the severe near-Arctic conditions. The native peoples reserved their affection, if any, for the lead dog, to whom the rest of the team gave allegiance. Because of such treatment, the modern Samoyed continued to have no trace of subservience. They command respect and reserve their whole-hearted cooperation for those who reciprocate. Not only did the dogs herd reindeer (their primary occupation), they also pulled sleds, accompanied their people on hunts for food, baby-sat children, and slept with the family to keep them warm. Some historians claim that these people cared so for their Samoyeds that they did not allow their dogs to mix with those of other groups traveling through the same area. This apparently contributed to the breed's retention of its original attributes for hundreds of years.

Samoyeds love children. Austin Michael deBack (great granson of
Agnes Mason) and Czar Nicholas (ten months old)

Photo courtesy of Pat deBack

How long has the Samoyed breed existed? Exciting new evidence
has emerged which demonstrates that the dogs may have been extant
more that five thousand years ago, a figure that replaces the traditional
scholarly speculation that dated the breed to approximately 1000
B.C.E.

A recently excavated burial site in Kazakhstan, dated 3500 B.C.E.,
has revealed the same practices and rituals seen in burial areas on the
Russian steppes from the Bronze and Iron Ages. The deceased were
buried with objects and belongings intended for use in the afterlife.
Also buried with them were their dogs, which were integral to human
survival.

Sandra L. Olsen, Ph.D., who discovered the skeletons of these dogs,
described her findings in an article, "Beware of Dogs Facing West,"
published in the magazine *Archaeology* (vol. 53, no. 4, July-August
2000). Curator of the Carnegie Museum of Natural History in Pitts-
burgh, Pennsylvania, Dr. Olsen works at dig sites during the summer.

During an interview, she told this author that the stature and cranial features of the skeletal remains resembled those of primitive Samoyeds more than any other breed of dog. This discovery may prove that the Samoyeds are a much older breed than originally estimated— by perhaps as much as four thousand years.

Surviving books tell tales of the Samoyed's incredible deeds. The breed was adept at rescue and finding obliterated trails. They were often sent alone to round up wild reindeer and herd them back to camp. The breed is said to have built up its amazing intellect at such times, because the dog would have to think for itself and make its own decisions. The Samoyed would sometimes be away from its camp for several days.

One account tells of a musher who fell through the ice when crossing a frozen river. His lead dog quickly sized up the situation and led the team cautiously to the very edge of the broken ice so the man could grab a sled runner. The team then pulled him free.

Recent visitors to an Alaskan village reported that every Samoyed there (most families had one or more) would howl in unison for exactly one minute, nonstop, beginning at precisely 11 p.m. One dog—who obviously kept the wristwatch—would sound off, with the rest instantly following suit. This is a manifestation of their ancestors' blood surging through their veins. According to some old timers, Samoyeds howled after dark, when the hunt began, and again when dawn was breaking, signifying the end of the hunt.

Should you decide that a Samoyed is the dog for you, you will come to appreciate the efforts of the ancient nomadic people who, under extremely adverse conditions, kept and nurtured the fascinating breed we enjoy today. Those of us who own and love this breed are obligated to continue the same careful and wise stewardship at all costs. Our turn is here and now.

Busboy...er, girl...um, dog?

Lisa Peterson's inventive Samoyed, Gefreda Twice Upon A Dream, made her own fun with the dishwasher. When her folks returned home from work each day, they were astounded to find all the dishes removed, taken out through the doggie door, and placed in the backyard. At first Lisa accused her husband of not closing the dishwasher. He repeatedly insisted he did. Finally Dream was seen opening the door herself. She emptied the dishwasher a number of times, says Lisa, and never broke a thing.

Chapter 4

Samoyed Speech

Do you ever get the feeling that you're living in a monkey house at the zoo some days? Do you think you're sharing space with Harpo Marx—someone having everything but the horn?

Then you have one or more Samoyeds! The big difference is that Harpo was silent. Samoyeds are not.

One day, with vitamin pills at the ready, I asked Pixie, "Where is Thompson?"

"I-oh-no," she replied immediately, with an interested eye on the pills. She would happily snap up his pill as well as her own, since she considers them a number one treat. I almost staggered backward. It is time to go public with this, I thought. Come to think of it, that's the way the Texas tongue pronounces "I don't know" on the laziest days. Any number of times, she has replied "I-oh-no" when asked "Where is your leash? Where is your chewbone? Where is Remington?"

Any dog that is a close companion and observes one's household habits will begin to understand the meaning of words—if spoken to about what is going on. Body language reinforces the verbal.

During routine activities, use set expressions along with consistent intonations to encourage your Samoyed to start imitating you. For instance, when you two get in the car, say "Hop in," or when going out a door, say "Let's go." If you tune in to your dog's wavelength, you might be surprised to find that he is imitating some of the words you say. Listen for words and short phrases.

Ch. Starshine's Wesson O'Pixie. Wesson, of the Seven Samurai, participates in flyball, obedience, weight pull, and some canine freestyle (dancing).

He is trained by owner Carol Brown.

The conversation may seem one-sided at first, but as one of the northern breeds known for communicating with howls and "w-o-o-o-o-o"s, your Sam may surprise you one day. He will probably speak in vowels, which are much easier for him to verbalize than consonants because of his different oral structure.

Attempts at speech are easier to detect when the dog imitates the intonation as well as pronunciation. You will be overjoyed when what he says fits in with what is happening. Praise him lavishly if you detect the faintest effort. For example, when he wants to go outdoors, he may stand by the door and say the equivalent of "Let's go!" He understands what it means.

When Fanya joined her family at four months of age, she was taken out before daybreak each morning for a quick run. Her handler would chirp "Let's go!" cheerily, despite the fact that she was half asleep. In a few weeks, Fanya was heard to say "Eh-h-oh," with the same intonation. After working on the hard **g** for several months, Fanya finally burst out with it one morning.

She continued to say it clearly all her life, and her puppies learned early to imitate her. They appeared to understand what it meant—

when they heard the phrase spoken, they would run to the back door, ready to exit. One pup, Rocky, would sit in front of the refrigerator and say "Let's go," hoping the door would be opened so he could get a treat.

Owners of some Samoyeds report their dogs say words clearly enough to be understood readily.

Astrid says "Hello" and "I love you," the latter coming out as "I uv ooo."

Winnie said "Hello" (with a little bow)…"Out!"…and "No!"

Tanta says "Out!"…"No!"…and "I do' (dough) wanna!"

Tanka (pronounced Than-ka) says "I do' wanna!"

Blue would fuss about being left at home, then say "I uv ooo" (you).

Pixie says "Ess go!"…"I oh no"…and "Do' (dough) wah 'at" (when offered food she does not want).

Fanya's speech included "Ess go!"…"No!"…and "Wah go ow!" (out).

Thompson (as do his siblings, mother, and grandmother) says "Ess go!"…"Go! Go! Go!" when he really wants action, and "Ball! Ball! Ball!" when looking for a game of toss. When he said words that were not understood by his human, he earnestly repeated them. If he had no success in making himself clear, he would simply walk away in frustration.

When a person in Spicy's family calls to another, she chimes in with something not yet completely correct, but having the same number of syllables. She is on the way to surprising her folks one day when she gets it right.

Listen to your Sam and tell him what a good dog he is when he attempts to speak. He may be hoping that you'll start paying attention to his remarks.

The Generation Gap?

When Pixie and her son, Thompson, are each given a biscuit bone, he preferred to hold and admire his a bit before eating it. Pixie would devour hers quickly then race, barking, to the back door. Thompson would immediately drop his bone and run to help catch the intruder Pixie implied was there. She would double back quickly, snatch up his treat, and bolt it down as well.

Chapter 5

Career Choices

Obedience

You will begin to think of obedience training pretty soon after you bring a puppy into your home. The puppy will remind you. Because a well-trained dog is a pleasure to have around and welcome everywhere, you will want to start teaching the fundamentals of good manners early on.

Begin as soon as possible. Start by teaching the pup what "Puppy come!" means. You may need this soon; it could save his life. Learning not to run out the door without your permission is equally important. Navigating on a leash, and, of course, catching on to the potty routine are also target behaviors. Do not allow the puppy to chew on your hands. He will think this is acceptable behavior, and chew on other peoples' hands. Stuff a toy in his mouth instead, and be sure that it is a toy that is safe for him to chew. Speaking of hands, never punish the puppy with your hand. He should always perceive it as being kind.

Teaching these behaviors as soon as possible is important. If your pup does not become accustomed to these actions from humans, he will cringe when the judge touches him if he is shown later. Instruct others who want to pet him to do so—with clean hands—under the chin or on the chest, not on top of his head. Something coming down on top of a dog's head is threatening to him.

Incorporating hand signals simultaneously with verbal commands is a wise approach. If for any reason you want to work with him in silence, he will understand. Also, the reinforcement may help him to learn more quickly. For example, a good time to give a hand signal is when you have given a treat to your puppy, and he begs for more. Hold up your empty hands and say "That's all!" He will turn his attention to something else. The same signal will also work on a drooling mob, if you have taught them correctly.

Always be calm, patient, consistent, and positive. These are also the characteristics you'll want to look for in an obedience teacher, should you wish to enroll your pup in classes. After your puppy's home-schooling, he will benefit from a class in which he will be exposed to more complex work, other people, and other dogs as part of his socialization.

Only after your puppy has had all his shots, however, would you consider taking him to a class. Even then, he may be too young to start. Read up on the subject, confer with obedience teachers, and/or audit their classes. Take a list of questions with you, and make notes of the responses. Talk to others whose dogs have taken obedience classes and will share their experiences with you. Do a lot of research before you decide on a class. Remember, your young Sam's attitude can be ruined by the wrong sort of treatment in an obedience class. Avoid instructors who advocate using the ear pinch to get the correct response; seek out teachers who use only positive reinforcement.

If your Samoyed is interested in and challenged by such classes, you and he may decide to go after some obedience titles. A dog well versed in obedience training has a leg up on other careers, such as search and rescue, flyball relay, agility, canine freestyle (dancing), drug detection, and service dog work. He can easily go on to more advanced pursuits, should you both choose. Think what fun you two will have then!

A great example of self-teaching one's dog is that of Mrs. Frank Butler, who was better known as Annie Oakley. She taught her hunting dog, an English Spaniel named Dave, to sit quietly on a tall stool while she shot an apple off his head. Dave would then leap down from his perch, grab the pieces, and toss them about in a dance of his own invention. Sometimes she would use an orange instead. She would also shoot in two a stick of chalk that Dave obediently held between his teeth. Annie and Dave worked together in the shooting exhibitions she frequently gave that so amazed audiences. Her dog was an integral part of her act.

This chapter will describe some of the activities and occupations available to Samoyeds. Not only do these dogs tend to excel at such pursuits, they are also exceptional ways to harness a Samoyed's intelligence and energy.

Herding

By Sharon Parker

The training arena gives my Sams a chance to pull surprises on me, bait me, and play their favorite game, "Gotcha!" with twinkling eyes. In a short time, they learn that they are safe from correction in the ring, and then it's time for "Gotcha!" They have a real sense of humor.

I will show a Samoyed a command as many times as needed to get a consistent response. I want him to achieve a strong connection to the command and respond with specific behavior. Then we build on that foundation. For example, the dog will learn to sit on command in

Sharon Parker and her Samoyed working on herding skills.

Photo by Kathy Madden

Louis Thompson, of Omega Samoyeds, and his dog sharpening herding skills.

Courtesy of Louis Thompson

different locations, not just the same familiar ones. The dogs that I herd will be taken to as many different training locations as possible before we go to a trial. This gives them exposure to new stock and facilities, different people, and unusual terrain. If the dogs work with the same sheep over and over, the sheep get to know the dog's strengths and weaknesses, and vice versa.

The hardest part about training is keeping the sessions short and brisk. It is hard to drive fifty miles for a herding lesson, then work for only ten or fifteen minutes. In the long run, however, the short sessions usually have more impact.

The Samoyeds get so creative in their training sessions that I try to mix it up for them. For example, I will teach different ways of getting to heel position. The dogs have to pay attention to do what I ask of them. A great deal of time is also spent on attention work. I watch the dog's ears more than I do his eyes. A good stock dog will be watching his stock but listening to his handler. He must keep an eye either on the animals or where he is going.

I don't allow any of that Samoyed "selective hearing" to come into play, either! When one starts to play that game, I get to that dog as quickly as I can and show up in his face. That gets his attention. The dog's reaction is "Wow! Where did she come from? I guess I'd better not do that again!"

Be consistent when training. If you want straight sits from Fido each time, do not let him get away with crooked ones. However, do try to keep training fun for the dog. There is nothing wrong with a game of fetch or some general play during a work session. It's fun for you and your four-legged partner. And remember, spectators love to watch a happy dog.

We start herding training by teaching our toddlers the sit, the down, and the stand commands. We use food rewards at this stage and do not position them with our hands. This technique makes the puppy use specific muscles for each particular action. Also, dogs that are introduced to learning at a young age seem to be willing learners for life.

Not all dogs place highly in competition, but they give you everything they can. So love and appreciate them for themselves. There are no special techniques—just time, patience, consistency, a little understanding, and lots of love.

Samoyed Herding Awards

In the early nineties, the AKC approved Samoyeds for competition in herding events. After all, herding was one of their jobs in the early days with the Samoyede people, along with sledding, hunting, and guarding. Listed here are the names of a few Samoyed achievers in this sport.

- Louis Thompson's Villan was the first Samoyed to earn the HS (Herding Started) title.

- Sharon and Dave Parker's Ch. Shada's Dancer of Tarahill CDX HS was the first Sam to be awarded High in Trial (the equivalent of Best In Show).

- Barb Cole's Barron was the first Samoyed to win the coveted OTCH (Obedience Trial Champion) title.

- Jan and Ann Schlobohm's Jake was first to get the first leg on his intermediate herding title.

Sledding

Agnes Mason's famous dog sled team driven by Lloyd Van Sickle, a noted musher. Rex is the lead dog. This team won the 2-day Sierra Dog Derby races at Truckee, California.

Alice Thompson Lombardi starts conditioning her sled dogs on a beach by October of each year. So does Tom Witcher. Before the winter snows hit, the teams train using sleds that are specially fitted with wheels instead of runners.

Alice says that a team can be composed of both male and female Samoyeds. However, when one of the girls comes into season, she cannot go sledding until it is over. When asked whether the males fight, Alice stated that as long as they were focused on work, the dogs did not squabble. They tended to business.

One race that Alice and her team were in was cancelled when a raging blizzard blew in. Unfortunately, she and the dogs were on a mountain. Alice put the team of five into her station wagon, tied the sled on top, and started down through the snow and ice. Suddenly, she was crowded off the road by another vehicle and found herself not only stuck, but also blocking the rest of the traffic trying to off the mountain safely.

Alice, with the help of several observers, struggled in vain to dislodge the station wagon. Seeing that these attempts were fruitless, she jumped out of the car and hitched the dogs to the front bumper. Her team, lead by the skillful Ch. Barchenok's Desire, promptly pulled the car back onto the narrow icy road, then on down to safer ground. Needless to say, the team got steak that night.

Mrs. Lombardi and her husband later flew to Fairbanks, Alaska, and took a river tour on a paddleboat named *The Discovery*. They were surprised when it stopped near the home of Susan Butcher, the second woman to win the Iditarod (Libby Riddles was the first). The highlight of their trip turned out to be meeting Mrs. Butcher and her husband, and getting to see their puppies. They were later told that the river was only forty-three inches deep, and froze solid in the winter. This provided ample testing ground for mushers and their teams.

When discussing sledding and Samoyeds, the name and influence of the remarkable Mary Agnes Bauer Mason cannot be overlooked. Her dedication to and expertise in the breed have had an enormous impact that continues to the present day.

Agnes Mason brought to California some of the first Samoyeds in America. She established what would later become the famous White Way Kennel, the foundation of which was five outstanding dogs from as many breeders. These Samoyeds were only a generation or two removed from the Samoyeds who survived the Polar expeditions. Mrs.

Exercising wheel invented and used by Mrs. Mason. Built by Jack Englert and on exhibit at the Fresno District Fair Annual Dog Show.

Courtesy of Pat deBack

"Stretching for a Tidbit"

Ch. Czar Nicholas LeBanof, part of Mrs. Mason's famous Samoyed team, with Mrs. Mason.

Courtesy of Sandra Flettner

Mason began and continued a breeding program that still influences the breed strongly today.

Mrs. Mason was also instrumental in establishing the breed standard, organizing exhibitions, and educating others about the proper care and treatment of the Samoyed. She even invented a huge exercise wheel that she used to condition her dogs. It is similar to the type seen in hamster cages.

Growing up in Alaska, Mrs. Bauer became well-versed in racing sled dogs because of her father's participation in the sport. She later trained what became known as her "famous sled dog team." This remarkable group of dogs won most long races, often beating Malamute and Husky teams—to the surprise of their mushers. The Sams' stamina was unbelievable.

In shorter races (those of about seventeen miles), the Samoyeds did not always win because they did not start by sprinting for a short distance. For centuries, their work had required them to maintain a steady pace for hours. It has been said that Samoyeds of good conformation and in good health can pull a load all day long, ending the day as fresh as they were at the beginning.

Incidentally, the expression "pound by pound" is used in the sport of sledding. What this means is that the winner of a race is determined by the weight of the dogs. The sled loads are all of the same weight, but the weight of the dogs, of course, varies. For example, a dog weighing eighty-five pounds who was pulling a thousand pounds would have pulled more weight than a dog weighing a hundred pounds who had also pulled a thousand pounds. Thus, the lighter dog would have expended the greater effort, and that would make him the winner.

In the mid-fifties, when a Southern Pacific train headed eastward to Reno and Chicago became snowbound, all sled dogs at a nearby (cancelled) show were called into action. For three or four days, the teams hauled supplies in to passengers and transported out those who were ill. The "famous sled dog team" participated in this effort, recalls Pat deBeck, a granddaughter of Agnes Mason. (Another granddaughter of Mrs. Mason, Sandie Flettner, contributed the information on "pound for pound" that is noted above.)

Mrs. Mason's teams had always helped out in emergency situations, so naturally when the newly formed Army K-9 Corps called for volunteers in 1942, she offered her Samoyeds for service. They were eager four-footed soldiers that became parachuters in the Parapups Battalion.

Mrs. Mason's famous Samoyed dog team, California State Fair, Sacramento, 1941.
Photo used on a calendar she had made and sent to friends with season's greetings at Christmas.

Courtesy of Pat deBack

Mrs. Mason and Aljean Mason with Samoyeds at Christmas.

Courtesy of Sandra Flettner

The Masons' 1943 Christmas card featured a photograph of her famous sled team. She included the following characteristics of the Samoyed: "Can always be trusted with those they know; good watchdogs but not vicious; easily trained; makes an excellent child's companion; independent but eager to learn; and should not be driven but taught." She added that "brushing with infrequent baths is all that is necessary to keep his beautiful appearance." She pointed out also that (a Samoyed) "should never be punished severely. The tone of voice is usually all that is necessary to control them." She obviously understood the character, intellect, and temperament of this distinctive breed.

In October 1961, admiring fellow members of the Samoyed Club of America, Pacific Coast Division, presented her with a framed list of her twenty-five champions. The heading of the honorific read "To Mrs. Agnes Mason in appreciation for her great devotion to the Samoyed Breed." That sentence says it all.

Agility

Mastering the obstacles in the varied arrangements of an agility course may be the type of challenge that a Samoyed craves.

Agility classes can alleviate the breed's "been there, done that" syndrome. The apparatus involved in this total exercise, such as the weave poles, A-frame, see-saw, and tire jump should pique his interest. If he is engaged by this sport, he will enjoy coping with the challenges and be eager to display his expertise, streaking through the equipment just for the fun of it. The excitement of his handler running with him, or attempting to do so, and the applause and encouragement from the spectators may spur him on to greater heights. The sight of this striking dog with the flowing white coat soaring through the obstacles, with his legs outstretched and tail waving, a big smile on his face, is truly thrilling.

Placing the jumps, dog walk, and other obstacles in a variety of patterns will keep your Sam on his toes, remembering, deciding, and doing. It may be the very sport that will challenge his quick mind. It is tailor-made for the dog who loves to do things.

Norma Pinkert and Levi

Courtesy of Scott Vail, Photographer

Ch. Donnereign Nakawes Taxiwa, AX, AXJ, aka "Taxi" zips through the weave poles in an Agility Trial.

Photo courtesy Tien Tran and Liz Kuivinen

"Taxi" jumping hurdles in an Agility Trial. She is owned and trained by Liz Kuivinen

Courtesy of owner

Lisa Peterson and Fancy

Courtesy of Scott Vail, Photographer

Liz Kuivinen and Tashe

Courtesy of Scott Vail, Photographer

Your Samoyed has as good a chance as any other breed at excelling, aided by his innate athletic ability that is sometimes overshadowed by the fluffy coat and occasional spells of ennui. The Sam's speed, stamina, and agility are so tested in few other sports. The exercise is good for his handler, too!

Books and/or classes by experts in this sport will get a dog and his owner started safely and correctly. As always, the dog's well-being and happiness are most important when considering any activity.

In November 1999, the first Samoyeds allowed to enter the AKC Agility Championships International earned their MX (Master Agility) titles. They are listed here with their titles and owners' names.

- Tamkobe Icetrix MX MXI (Kylie Bourke)
- Ch. Donnerreign Nakawes Taxiwa AX AXJ (Liz Kuivinen)
- Silveracres Fantasee CD AX AXJ (Lisa Peterson)
- Tzar's New Ad-Venture AX AXJ (Norma Pinkert)

Flyball Relay Races

Flyball Relay is a fast-growing and fast-moving sport for dogs that is as exciting for participants as it is for spectators. The audience cheers on its favorites, willing them to move faster and win! The competition in this team sport is fierce, and the dogs streak by with flying legs that scarcely touch the ground.

The racing course is set up with a series of four jumps and a special "box." Each team has up to six dogs on it, four to run and two as alternates. The dogs are held at the start/finish line by their owners.

"Poppy," the #1 Flyball point-scoring Samoyed in the World

Crosswinds Spirit's SE-Duck-Tion C.D., T.T., C.G.C, T.D., F.C.H.

Photos courtesy of Kathy Kennedy

One dog at a time races down the lane, leaps over the four jumps (which are set ten feet apart) and hits a paddle or other part of the box that releases a tennis ball. He catches the ball and races back over the jumps with it, dropping it only when he reaches the start/finish line. The second the first dog reaches the start/finish line, the next dog races off to do the same thing. When he returns, the third and fourth dogs follow suit one at a time. While this team is racing, there is another team next to it doing the same thing. The dogs must be trained to focus on the business at hand and ignore the others. The team whose fourth dog crosses the finish line first wins the race.

The dogs are all running and leaping over two-foot-wide jumps at top speed. No fencing or barrier of any kind is placed between the lanes. The action is fast and furious. Spectators have to look quickly or they miss the entire race!

An extremely fast time for all four dogs to finish a race is seventeen seconds. The average time is in the twenty to twenty-four second range. The lane is a hundred and two feet long, which means that the dogs run four hundred and eight feet (don't forget the four jumps) in less than seventeen seconds.

Sometimes (during a demonstration instead of a serious race), for variety as well as the amusement of the ringsiders, a short-legged dog is added to a team of larger dogs. One can almost hear the observers willing it over the obstacles. The crowd roars with delight if the disgusted little dog runs around the jumps—or simply washes his paws of the dilemma and leaves.

Kathy Kennedy's dog, Poppy (Crosswinds Spirit's Se-Duck-Tion CD TT CGC), has accrued more flyball points than any other Samoyed in the world. It may be hard to believe, Kathy says, but most dogs can learn flyball in a short time. It helps, she adds, if they are "ball crazy."

Kathy states that all an owner needs to do to begin flyball training is play tennis ball games with your puppy, doing a lot of restrained recalls. Puppies can start going over four-inch-high jumps at about seven or eight months of age. If you can get him to carry a ball over the jump, you will already have a head start when you begin flyball classes. She suggests getting a good book about the sport for an explanation of the game as well as training tips.

Juno and Poppy

Kathy and Nick Kennedy are a wonderful example of people who give their multi-talented Samoyeds opportunities to participate in a variety of activities. Not only have their dogs had fun and also excelled in any sports they have participated in, but their growing family has also bene-fitted. The Kennedys have balanced their family routine and activities important to their growing children with participation in dog sports.

"I have divided my weekends among many activities," Kathy explained. "Juno was my foundation bitch. She got her championship easily with four majors and the CD in three shows. We had her before we had children. She went everywhere with us." When Juno was five, the Kennedys had their first child, followed by two more. All three loved to crawl in Juno's crate to nap with her.

"Juno" (Ch. Tarahill's Arctic Delight, CD, TT, CGC) about ten feet off the ground on a large oak limb.

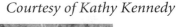

Courtesy of Kathy Kennedy

"Juno" in Uniform
Ch. Tarahill's Arctic Delight

Courtesy of Kathy Kennedy

Juno is also a therapy dog who has helped severely handicapped children. When she was about seven, she began to do something that is rather strange—especially for a dog.

The family moved to a house with a huge oak tree in the yard. The lowest limb was more than six feet from the ground. One day, Juno

Poppy as a pup (9 weeks) with "Uncle Stuffer" (Ch. Crosswinds The Right Stuff) and three-year-old Rachel Kennedy.

chased a squirrel, which tried to elude her by running up the oak tree. Imagine that squirrel's surprise (and alarm) when Juno continued to chase it up the tree! From then on, she spent every minute she could up in that tree. She managed to climb up to limbs that were ten to fifteen feet off the ground, obviously enjoying her view of the world from her private perch.

Juno died at age sixteen, but had lived a good life and entertained her admirers with her astonishing antics.

Poppy (Crosswinds Spirit's SE-Duck-Tion CD TT CGC) is Juno's granddaughter, sired by Ch. Kazakh's Lucky Duck. At eight years of age, she has already earned her Therapy Dog, Temperament Tested, Companion Dog, and Flyball Champion titles. She is conformation pointed and a BOB (Best of Breed) winner.

Poppy's flyball training sessions were given intermittently over a number of years because of an Achilles tendon injury, her seasons, and Kathy's inability to take her to flyball competitions. She had a total of about eight months of training spread over three years. Even though she has attended a limited number of flyball tournaments, she has accumulated more points than any other Sam in the world.

Poppy and her pal and flyball partner, Deva the Whippet, all hugged up and catching some zzz's.

Courtesy of Kathy Kennedy

Canine Musical Freestyle

An exciting new sport in the dog world, Musical Freestyle, is spreading across the country like wildfire. Each program demonstrating this amazing collaboration between handler and dog boosts its popularity. Audiences applaud wildly after every performance. Musical Canine Sports International, the Canadian group organized to develop and promote this sport, describes it as a "blending of dog obedience and dance that presents a visually exciting display of handler and canine teamwork."

Musical Freestyle is dancing to music with one's dog. Obedience movements, plus a variety of others, are incorporated into a choreographed routine that features the handler's interpretation of the music.

Pepper dances with her owner/trainer, Sandra Davis. Pepper is a top winner—the expresion on her face is priceless!

An obedience competitor and teacher, credited with train ing six dogs who received their OTCH, Sandra Davis became interested in Musical Freestyle after reading an article about it in 1994. With her background in ballet and obedience instruction, she was a natural to become involved in this competitive sport.

With her Border Collie, Pepper, and her Giant Schnauzer, Jabba (short for Jabberwocky), she has given stunning performances before enthusiastic audiences in the U. S. and Canada. She has been interviewed and profiled in numerous publications, serving as an ambassador for this new activity.

Sandra, who lives in El Paso, Texas, has made three excellent videos that gradually increase in skill level. With such instruction, owner and dog can both learn the techniques at home and benefit from Sandra's expertise. As interest in Canine Freestyle gathers momentum, classes are becoming available in more areas.

The following interview with Sandra will be helpful to anyone who wants to get started in Musical Freestyle, or just wishes to understand the complexities involved in performance.

Can just anyone do it?

You need a dog that will respond to motivational training, as well as an owner who will do what is necessary to train the dog for performance. Training a dog to perform a group of moves on cue is not easy. Infinite patience, consistent commands, and diligence are needed. The reason freestyle started in the obedience community is because experienced trainers had dogs that were used to responding to training. I'm a professional trainer. Could pet owners do it with their dog? Probably, to some extent.

Is it better to be in a class or teach your dog alone?

Experienced dog trainers would probably do better alone, rather than being held back by a class. If one is inexperienced, a class is definitely better.

Should a dog have obedience training first?

In my opinion, yes, but it depends on the person's goals. For public performances, a dog is needed that will not become distracted by anything when dancing, that will perform within the context of the routine, and will appear to be enjoying every minute. This requires a rather high level of obedience training first, at least through CDX work.

Can the dog be taught a few essentials along with the dance moves?

This depends on the dog, the owner, and the goal. The most difficult transition in teaching freestyle is removing the hand cues and getting the dog to do a move with just a word. It requires some physical guidance and good timing in praising even the dog's tiniest attempt at the move.

Should the dog learn all the moves before using music?

In dancing, one has to learn a movement before performing a routine. I devised twenty basic moves, teaching them to Pepper until she would do each of them on voice cue alone. This means no hand cues, body cues, or music cues. Once she learned them that well, I could tell how fast she would be able to do them. Then I could think about the rhythm and beat for our music. Pepper does nothing slowly, so I choose my music according to her response time. Since she could do the moves on voice cue, I was free to use my hands and body to express my part in the routine. My hands, body, and the music then become cues for all the moves, as well as the context of the moves. Pepper knows ten different dances, and can keep them all straight because of the context. Most of our moves are in every dance somewhere, but she does not get confused.

Many more moves have been developed from the basic twenty. Once a dog knows only six or seven moves, enough to put in a dance, a routine should be constructed so that there is completion of a dance goal, and the dog can experience success by performing the dance. Constantly teaching moves without performing a dance is not very rewarding for dog or handler, and is stressful for both. Success with a complete, simple dance routine makes the training enjoyable. Everything that follows should be easier and come faster.

Does your training use a positive mode? How about rewards?

Positive? Yes! For rewards, I use a tug rope for Pepper and a tennis ball for Jabba.

Pepper is motivated by anything I do with her; that is why I bought a Border Collie. Jabba does nothing for free, and as little as he can for rewards. I food trained him in obedience and played a lot of ball with him for exercise. I used the ball to teach him dance, and it worked fine.

Do you teach moves in a certain order?

No, but I work on many at the same time. Circle moves are the easiest and most fun, so I use all of them each session. However, I also work on harder parallel moves, moving backward and forward in front of me, and the side passes with me that are the most difficult and least fun for the dog. Repeating the name of each move a lot helps the dog identify it.

On the average, how long does it take a dog to learn routines for a performance?

It depends on the dog, the handler, and the amount of time spent. From experience, I can tell you that it took me six months to teach Pepper twenty moves and polish her first dance routine to performance quality. However, she is a very special dog who was trained through AKC utility exercises before we started, even though she was only thirteen months old at the time. I worked with her two or three times every day.

How long should a dance last?

If it is the first dance for dog and handler, I'd say ninety seconds, maximum. I don't like to repeat moves a lot. Each dance should be as long as it takes for the dog to do the moves that it knows no more than twice. Audiences get bored with repetition. My second tape explains how to shorten songs. It is impossible to find the right music that runs under three minutes.

Do you use any special props for training or dancing?

I use dowels to teach the dog position on the parallel moves. I use a plunger, since it will stand by itself, to teach the dog to circle a cane, which will be used in some dances. Many plungers with rope attached make an aisle to teach the dog to back away from me about twenty to thirty feet. In dances I use only a cane.

Any advice on costumes for dog and partner?

Yes, I definitely like costumes, but simple ones. Use only neckwear for the dogs. People can wear anything that feels comfortable. Costumes make it more entertaining, and can make one feel less self-conscious.

Do you prefer certain types and tempos of music?

Yes. I want highly identifiable songs, those I think my audience will know and like, that have a beat or tune that is catchy and uplifting. My dances are light and burlesque. I want the audience to laugh along with us. I like parody.

A person needing help with choreography could contact a local ballet teacher. Be sure the dog knows all the moves you want to use first. Dance studios have slick floors, so you may need to choose another location for rehearsals.

Have you heard of any Samoyeds performing in Canine Freestyle?

No, I haven't. But they're such pretty dogs, they would make a nice dance picture. (Author's note: a Sam in Houston is now happily taking lessons, and several others are getting started. Remember, the Samoyed simply loves to do things. It does not seem to matter what!)

Are you planning to make a video of some performances for public entertainment?

Yes, I'm now working on a video of dances only. It will be accompanied by information about the dances themselves, where new moves were added, and how some of the more difficult moves were taught. Everyone wants to know how I taught Pepper to weave backwards. This video will include six of Pepper's dances, and maybe one with Jabba.

Sandra and Pepper are known as the Dancing Duo. She quit teaching competition obedience lessons to be free to travel and perform with Pepper. They have performed at the America's Family Pet Expo, the Calgary Stampede, the AstroWorld Series of Dog Shows, and at the Texas State Fair. They were filmed for the "Amazing Tails" program, shown on the Animal Planet network. They have also performed at the River City Cluster of Dog Shows in San Antonio.

Sandra spent eighteen years breeding and exhibiting Great Danes "along with a few Bassett Hounds and Welsh Corgis" in conformation, and ten years owning and showing American Saddlebred horses. She discovered obedience training and competition in 1981. Sandra is now one of the most respected experts and performers in Musical Freestyle.

Another noted performer is Carolyn Scott of Houston, who also teaches canine freestyle. She competed in obedience training for eighteen years, then became interested in Musical Freestyle when she saw a videotape of one of the first demonstrations. She has successfully competed in two major competitions. Her dog, Rookie, is now the only one to hold the title of MSXI, Musical Freestyle Dog Excellent. She and Rookie give unbelievable performances with extremely rapid footwork.

The first organization in the south, the Footloose Canine Freestyle Association, has been formed in Houston, Texas. It hosted the first Freestyle Event in the area, which was held in November, 1998.

For more freestyle information, write or call any of the following:

Canine Freestyle Federation
Joan Tennille
4207 Minton Drive
Fairfax, Virginia 22032
Phone 703 323 7216

A group organized to structure freestyle activities and competitions in the U.S.

Ventre Advertising Inc.
P O Box 350122
Brooklyn, New York 11235
Pati Ventre venad@aol.com

Coordinator of Pup-peroni Freestyle events. Sells tapes of the demos at Regionals and Classics.

Dancing Dogs Videos
P O Box 3324
El Paso, Texas 79923

Sandra Davis' videos: Series of three tapes of instruction, plus new tape of dances only

Carolyn Scott, Chairperson
7830 Whispering Wood
Houston, Texas 77086

Footloose Fantasy Freestyle Event

Musical Canine Sports International (MCSI)
Sharon Tutt, Treasurer/Membership Chair
16665 Parkview Place
Surrey, B.C. Canada V4N 1Y8

Dues ($20 annually) includes Rule Book, Guidelines, Scoring Manual, and six Newsletters

Service Dogs

Living with the disabling effects of the incurable neuromuscular disease myasthenia gravis (as well as arthritis) inspired Joan Froling to investigate how service dogs could assist persons with disabilities, to give them more independence and even the ability to travel. She acquired Nikki, a remarkable Samoyed, and had him trained to do some fifty tasks. He performed so well and willingly that she needed no other help.

Influential worldwide, Joan founded the International Association of Assistance Dog Partners. She also edits its quarterly newsletter, *Partners Forum*, which has been a five-time nominee for the Maxwell Award (the Dog Writers Association of America's equivalent of the Pulitzer Prize). She actively trains other service dogs with their partners. In October 1999, she was inducted into the National Hall of Fame For Persons With Disabilities in Columbus, Ohio.

Here is her touching story of Nikki, the service dog extraordinaire. Incidentally (and not surprisingly), this story won the 2001 Maxwell Award.

Choices of the Heart

By Joan Froling
Copyright September 11, 1999

Nikki was my first service dog. I didn't know what to expect of one, so it was only in retrospect I could see the forest for the trees and recognize this particular Samoyed was much too willful and independent to be an ideal service dog. He made up his own rules. Talked back to me and other people. Wasn't even affectionate. No doggy kisses. Didn't like hugs or cuddling. Rarely solicited petting. Preferred to sleep on the cool tiles in a hotel bathroom or stretch out in the front hallway at home, rather than next to my bed. The only times he lay at my feet and looked up at me with an adoring gaze were on the nights I had a pizza delivered.

Nikki carrying an item to the checkout counter.

All photos in this section courtesy of Joan Froling

I suspect most people are like my sister, preferring dogs that are demonstrative, wiggling with joy if praised, eager to give sloppy kisses or to climb into a lap if invited.

Nikki suited me just fine. He was a service dog, not a lap dog. As long as he did his job, his free time was his own time. The way I saw it, his love wasn't something to be measured by the number of doggy kisses he doled out per week but by every service dog task he performed. He had a choice in whether or not he would cooperate. He let me know it too.

I'll never forget the very first time I asked him to demonstrate a service dog task in front of somebody else. Our first audience was an old friend who dropped by. I had practiced with Nikki earlier that day and he was letter perfect. Whenever I said the word "Basket," he'd rush into the kitchen, open a cupboard door and bring me a straw basket containing prescription medication and a can of Diet Coke so I could wash the pills down. I figured this would be a very useful task on the days when I couldn't get up from the couch for six hours because I was receiving IV medication for my neuromuscular disease, myasthenia gravis. It also would be a wonderful convenience whenever I was in pain from the orthopedic complications that had taken quite a toll over the last fifteen years. My friend was very impressed when I told her what I had trained Nikki to do, especially after so many stories of his puppy-from-hell escapades during the first fourteen months of his life.

They say "pride goeth before fall." I confidently gave Nikki the command that afternoon, expecting him to dazzle my friend with his mastery of this complex new task.

Can you imagine how impressed my friend was when Nikki left the room and instead of returning with the basket, he came sauntering back in with a rawhide bone? He plopped himself down at my feet and began chewing on the rawhide bone with great relish. So much for Nikki, the Samoyed Wonder Dog. She thought it was hilarious. She tried not to giggle but couldn't help herself.

I was shocked speechless. I knew this was not a case of forgetfulness. Especially when Nikki reacted to her giggle by lifting his head, grinning that Samoyed grin of his, then returned to earnestly chomping on the bone, making as much noise as possible.

Nikki had already taught me that he could not be guilt tripped like most dogs into complying with a command. You could try shaming

Nikki pulling Joan through a department store, going shopping.

him till hell froze over and the scolding would merely sail in one ear and out the other, not troubling his conscience the least little bit.

Nikki also knew he was much stronger than I. Physically dragging him into the kitchen to the cupboard where the basket awaited him was out of the question.

Repeating the command when he was pretending to have amnesia as to its meaning did not make much sense. I was not dealing with a confused dog. He was deliberately being a wiseguy.

After giving it some thought, I decided to see if I could re-direct his attention by putting on an act myself. I held out a milkbone. I pretended I was going to eat it. I made sounds indicating this was the most delicious yummy milkbone I'd ever seen. A feast!

Nikki stopped gnawing with exaggerated fervor on the rawhide bone. His head swiveled in my direction. His smug amusement at my expense began to wane. The sight of the milkbone was his undoing. He began salivating. He couldn't help it.

I continued to let him know this was the most delectable exquisite tidbit on the planet and if a certain youngster didn't hustle his bustle, the trainer was gonna eat the prize herself.

He looked down at the rawhide bone, then up at the milkbone, then stared at me as if to say, "oh, you're gonna fight dirty, huh?"

Our duel of wits ended when he abruptly decided to carry out the command without further ado. Whether it was hunger pangs or he merely wearied of the stunt he was pulling with the rawhide bone, I shall never know for sure.

Well, that was the beginning. Nobody said it would be easy to transform a Samoyed into Sir Galahad.

Two years later, in July 1993, Nikki and I gave another demonstration of service dog work, one I won't soon forget.

Before I go into the details, perhaps a few words about what led up to it would be in order. In 1991, I asked the United Way agency, Paws With A Cause, for "how to" information on teaching a certain skill. Two staff members, Lynn Hoekstra and Linda Brady, came to my home, did a "needs assessment," and suggested additional ways Nikki and I could learn to work together as a team to reduce my dependency on family members, conserve energy and enhance my safety. I decided

Dakota brings in the groceries.

to formally apply to their program for advanced task training. I will always be grateful for this help I received with Nikki's education. We became a certified team after six months of hard work. Some of the tasks Nikki and I learned from the field trainer, Linda Brady, like wheelchair pulling, opening heavy commercial doors, bringing in the groceries and fetching a portable phone in an emergency has made it feasible for me to live alone and to travel on my own. Thrilled by the results, I naturally wanted to help other disabled persons experience the dramatic improvement in quality of life that is possible through assistance dog partnership. One of the ways I went about it back then was to put on educational demonstrations with Nikki about the benefits of working with a service dog whenever invited to by Paws With A Cause or the United Way or the Oakland/Macomb Center for Independent Living.

The average audience is pretty unsophisticated but the one Nikki and I faced in July 1993 was at the opposite end of the scale. We had been asked to appear at the World Series of Dog Obedience, a prestigious annual tournament which attracts top obedience teams from across the USA. The PAWS field trainer who helped Nikki and me to reach our full potential as a team wanted to demo the most unusual, difficult and interesting of the fifty tasks Nikki had mastered to date. She hoped it would inspire some of the top obedience trainers in the country at that event to consider taking on the challenges and rewards of becoming a service dog trainer.

The potential downside was that if Nikki screwed up in front of this audience, it would reflect badly on the program's reputation in the obedience world, not just embarrass his owner into becoming a hermit. It was one of the few times I was nervous going into a demo.

Have you ever had one of those horrible days when nothing seems to go right? Nikki vomited that morning. I was in a quandary over whether or not to cancel. When we arrived at the arena, PAWS volunteers were waiting in the parking lot to rush me inside, no time to let Nikki "visit a bush" on the way in. No time to confer with Linda Brady about him possibly being sick. Instead of being able to give Nikki at least an hour to adjust to the strange building, barking dogs, multiple odors and crackling PA System, we were suddenly "on." Unexpectedly, the judging had finished way ahead of schedule.

I needn't have worried. Nikki sailed through this showcase of tasks with flying colors. His laid back, amiable mood didn't waver till the very end.

To illustrate to the audience how Nikki can fetch the medicine basket out of my kitchen cupboard, on days when I get my IV medication, Linda had suggested we put his yellow basket inside a dog crate, the plastic kind that airlines use. I sent him to open the crate door with a tug on a string and to retrieve the heavy basket that held two cans of Diet Coke and several prescription bottles. His delivery couldn't have been more courteous. Unfortunately, when I asked Nikki to demo the task "Shut the Cupboard Door," by having him shut the crate door, I discovered there's a price to pay for complacency. I never thought to ask Nikki to practice on a crate door before. We were about to learn that a kitchen cupboard door stays closed when Nikki butts it with his nose. A crate door bounces right back open.

I still remember the puzzlement in Nikki's eyes as he headed back to me, for he did not hear the familiar words of praise he was expecting. I didn't know if I should take a big chance, ask him to do the task over, or shrug off this failure. I decided to gamble. Taking a deep breath, I pointed to the wire mesh crate door and asked him to shut it.

Nikki was surprised. He put on the brakes. He obediently returned and espying the problem, this time he gave the crate door a super hard butt with his nose, determined to slam it shut for good. He confidently wheeled around and came trotting back to me, certain he'd taken care of the dumb thing. When he heard the ripple of laughter go through the crowd, he didn't need me to tell him something was wrong.

Nikki hated being laughed at. He looked over his shoulder and let out a cry of pure frustration. The crate door was wide open again!

The crowd thought this was very funny. I could feel him seething inside as he returned to confront the problem. Then they fell silent, watching something they don't get to see too often with obedience competition dogs. They got to watch a working dog do problem solving on his own initiative.

Nikki studied the crate door for about five seconds. He experimentally gave the crate door a nose butt from the wrong side of the mesh to see what would happen. It swung in the wrong direction, came rebounding back to almost shut itself, then bounced back open.

Calmly, deliberately, Nikki walked around the crate door till he stood on the correct side. He gently nudged the mesh as if it were as fragile as an eggshell. The door advanced only an inch or two. He took a step, again gently nudging the door. He took a third step. He cautiously waited to see if the door would jump back at him, then nudged it once more. He continued to move the crate door at this carefully controlled pace till he finally had it shut.

Interestingly, for about seven seconds, Nikki didn't move. He prudently waited, ready to react if the crate door began to swing open. When he was finally satisfied he had completed the task I sent him to perform, he came for his praise. He was beaming from ear to ear. His proud step and the jaunty wave of his plumy tail signaled "Mission Accomplished."

Nikki received a standing ovation from the audience. He stood quietly at my side, ready for the next command, a striking portrait of canine dignity and devotion to duty. It is a moment I have held in my heart for many years. It is one thing to persuade a dog to mind you in your own

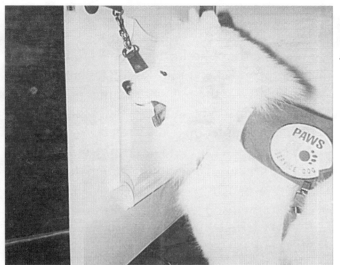

Nikki opening the front door for Joan.

living room where there are no distractions. It was quite another to put him into this kind of a public pressure cooker and demand he perform fifteen to twenty tasks in a row with nary a break in between. What a joy it was to have a Samoyed like this one for a partner!

However, Nikki never let me take his cooperation entirely for granted. From time to time, he would indulge in a bit of deviltry that was absolutely fascinating. It began about a year and a half into our partnership. Significantly, it only occurred on dull boring evenings when we were alone and there was no particular urgency to the command I gave. He never goofed off if I wasn't feeling well. But just to make sure I didn't forget his cooperation was purely voluntary, that he still had a choice in the matter, on a quiet evening when I had my nose buried in a book or my writing, he would occasionally respond to my request in a way that couldn't be interpreted as confusion.

I would tell him to fetch a Diet Coke, a familiar task he carried out three or four times a day, week in and week out, without fail. Normally he'd be back in a jiff, a cold beverage from the refrigerator in his jaws, eager to turn it over. Once in a while though, I'd be startled to find Nikki delivering the Emergency phone to me. Giving him the benefit of the doubt, I'd repeat the request for the soda pop, using a hand signal in addition to the verbal cue. Nikki would dash over to the corner of the living room, grab my cane and drag it back, dropping it at my feet. I'd tell him to cut out the clowning and get me that pop! At that point he typically went in the opposite direction. He'd race to the front door, snag the tug strap attached to the lever handle and pull it open, letting in a swirl of cold air or the heat of a summer night, ignoring my protest. He'd pick up something on the way back...a slipper or a shoe. He'd quite deliberately saunter up to the wastebasket, dark eyes agleam with mischief. No matter what I said or didn't say, he'd dump the object into the wastebasket and stand there grinning that insolent Samoyed grin of his.

I admit I loved it! Intelligent disobedience—Samoyed style.

Sometimes people would ask how I could stand living with such a pushy dog. When Nikki wanted to go outside or wanted you to get up and let him back into the house, he'd make a vocal request. If you didn't pay attention, he'd get louder. If you continued to ignore him, he'd march up to you and tell you exactly what he thought of your attitude, his nose a mere six inches from your own. If outside, he'd bark. If you didn't hurry, he'd begin howling. He would not be ignored! Of course every time I gave in to him, it just reinforced his belief that this was an effective way to communicate his need. I thought his persistence was amusing, but people who occasionally babysat with him did not find it to be an endearing trait. I would defend him by pointing out he only asked two things of me each day—a bowl of food and a bathroom break now and then. Think of how many times a day I demanded "immediate service" from Nikki! He just wanted a little quid pro quo.

But they still grumbled, cutting him no slack. I found such pettiness hard to fathom. To be fair, they had no firsthand experience with Nikki's "good side." How he pulled my wheelchair through snow and slush, drenching rains and hot muggy weather with impeccable teamwork, heedless of his own discomfort. How he assisted me to the best of his ability when various medical problems occurred in public or at home. They hadn't toured museums full of art treasures, served on boards and commissions or participated in four international conferences in the assistance dog field thanks to his cooperation. They didn't appreciate that I'd been housebound for all practical purposes, unable to go any place alone before this partnership of ours. I guess it is all a matter of perspective.

I've heard it said your first service dog seems magical. Because of my background as a professional dog trainer and lifelong study of dog psychology, I could find a rational explanation for just about every-thing that occurred with Nikki and other dogs I've known or heard about. I have a fairly good grasp of a dog's capabilities and what you can realistically expect in any given situation. But admittedly there was one aspect of the relationship between Nikki and me that remains a mystery. It taught me to keep an open mind when I listen to others recount their experiences with an assistance dog.

Whenever I was in pain and needed something out of reach, some-thing I'd never asked for before or something I asked for so seldom, there was no command for it, I'd send Nikki to do what might be called "a blind retrieve." I'd indicate the general whereabouts of something, then with verbal cues and hand signals, play a game of "You're getting hotter…you're getting cold," to help the dog to zero in on the right object. Usually it involved getting something off the hotel room dresser or desk or my living room couch or the television, fireplace, stereo cabinet or another piece of furniture rather than the floor.

Nikki helping to unpack the groceries.

Dakota carries his pan for refill.

With my successor dog, Dakota, it can take up to ten minutes before he hits on the right item. There are times when I just have to give up and call off the quest. With Nikki, though, the results were uncanny. He'd almost always locate the item on the first or second try. If this had happened only once or twice, I would have chalked it up to sheer coincidence but it happened so often over the years, it defied logic.

One example that comes to mind is the time I needed a business card off the hotel dresser so I could cancel a dinner appointment due to being under the weather. The dresser was cluttered with milkbones, lifesavers, a dog leash, grooming utensils, toiletries, books, papers, pens, hotel literature and assorted other items. Nikki found the business card within three seconds. He ignored the milkbones, ignored all the more familiar objects I may have been seeking. It was an incredible thrill to experience this level of successful communication with a dog. It was not something I ever counted on, nor did I ever get upset if it didn't happen. I certainly don't expect it from future dogs. While scientists may explain it away as nothing more than a super acute reading of body language or a lucky guess, to me it will always be part of the special magic of that first partnership.

In 1993, my Samoyed became the first working service dog to earn the title of AKC Champion. Actually, the one who earned that title was his long suffering volunteer handler, Linda Brady, who refused to give up on his dog show career. Nikki didn't see why he should passively permit some stranger with a badge labeled "Judge," to pull back his lips and examine his teeth, squeeze his body parts and rumple his coat. What kind of dumb game was that? Nor did he like playing "statue," being forbidden to move one paw out of place for minutes at a stretch. His Samoyed sense of humor led him to experiment with ways to spice this game up, keep it interesting…

In 1994, I had the pleasure of watching Nikki compete at the Westminster Kennel Club dog show. It was to be the last of our glory days. He turned out to be one of those rare unfortunate dogs who x-ray free of hip dysplasia when under eighteen months of age, but go on to develop it later. By age four and a half, he began to show signs of occasional bouts of arthritic pain in one hip. I battled it with Adequan shots and herbal remedies, achieving temporary relief but not remission. By his sixth birthday, he needed a costly operation or a merciful shot to put him out of his misery.

Some decisions you make with your head, not your heart. Training a successor dog was an absolute necessity if I was to continue a life of public service. When the first one did not work out, I put him in a career change home and grimly started over from scratch.

With Nikki, my heart made the choices. I gave him the very expensive surgery. It brought him two pain free years and a fairly good quality of life in his final year. He received the best of care and special treats and extra attention. Since "retirement" was NOT a word in his vocabulary, I promoted him to the rank of "Professor." The first six months were rough sailing, but eventually we were able to work things out so he still felt useful and cherished, without putting Dakota's nose too far out of joint.

One way of putting Nikki's intelligence to good use was by introducing a laser pointer and other experimental devices to Nikki first, which helped me figure out the best way to teach something new to my successor dog or to a service dog candidate who would visit or board with us from time to time. I also utilized Nikki's skills by having him demonstrate a particular task before allowing the others to have a go at it. Professor Nikki soon learned he must allow other dogs, especially Junior [aka Dakota] to respond to my task commands, only intervening if it became clear the dog was too confused to figure out what I needed. Nikki became a tremendous asset in that respect.

On the last night of his life, Nikki lay in his favorite spot by the front door listening to me work with Dakota in the other room. I had asked Dakota to fetch the TV remote control off the top of the television set. Dakota lacks Nikki's terrific memory for word association. He may not have understood exactly what he was supposed to be looking for. He didn't think to look on top of the TV cabinet for the item, as it was over his head, above his line of sight. He kept passing right by the object I needed, again and again.

Hearing the exasperation in my voice, Nikki dragged his weak hindquarters across the tiled floor. When he reached the living room carpeting, which gave him some traction, he pulled himself to his feet in spite of the sharp pain this effort surely cost him. I was very surprised when he came into view. His health had deteriorated over the last several months to the point where he seemed to be too feeble to get up on his own. For the last four days, the only times he would get up were the times when I went in to physically aid him and to verbally insist he make the effort. Yet here he was!

It took Nikki all of five seconds to figure out the location of the TV remote control. He plucked it off the top of the television cabinet.

Dakota rushed up, snatched the remote control out of Nikki's jaws and came hustling over to me, insisting as usual that HE was the service dog in the family.

Nikki just looked at me, a tired smile in his eyes, bemused by Junior's rude behavior. He never took offense. He had been patiently showing Junior where to find things for nearly four years.

I'll never forget Nikki getting up like that to come to the rescue on our last evening together.

Some might say it was only a TV remote control. What's the big deal? A Hollywood scriptwriter would insist on changing the ending, wanting the dog to do something the public would recognize as heroic. Save me from a fire, an intruder, something melodramatic.

But that would not accurately reflect the real extent of Nikki's devotion to duty.

Dakota carrying basket of medications to Joan.

His courageous effort to overcome his painful infirmities so he could assist me that night sprang from the heart of a true service dog. No job too small. No letting me down because a task is boring or mundane. He couldn't grasp the difference between a remote control or an emergency telephone or some other object in terms of its importance, he only knew that I needed his help. He was there for me right up to the very end.

I was there for him, too. His quality of life had gone downhill to the point where it would not have been a kindness to keep him earthbound. I had promised him that afternoon, while comforting him after a fall, that "enough was enough" and I would let him go, even though the thought of saying goodbye to him was excruciating. I couldn't ask my best friend to keep working for me, even though he loved it and I loved having him here. There comes a day when the biological effects of the aging process or disease are irreversible and life no longer holds a promise of a better tomorrow. So I kept my word. The next morning, in the shade of an old fruit tree, with the help of a veterinarian, I released his magnificent spirit.

It was not an easy thing to do.

I held him for a long time afterwards, the warm sun on my face, the breeze ruffling his fur. I remembered the highlights of our journey

Dakota carrying Joan's cane to her.

together, a journey that had spanned nearly a decade. Along with the grief there was so much gratitude to the Powers-that-be, for Nikki's presence in my life, for all the new friends and opportunities that this partnership has brought my way.

It has taken me most of the summer to reach the point where I could finally write about the dog with the spectacular white coat and beautiful dark eyes who taught me about assistance dog partnership.

He may not have been everyone's idea of an ideal service dog. But when I think back on my partnership with Nikki, it is the humor, the gallantry and the magic that lives on in my memory. As willful and mischievous as he could be at times, whenever it really counted, he was my Sir Galahad. There will never be another like him.

Search and Rescue

According to Lynn Godbee of Sweetwater, Texas, her dog is the only Samoyed being trained to search for human bodies in bombed or collapsed buildings, train wrecks, tornado debris, or other disasters. She agrees that owners need to channel their Samoyed's intelligence, or they are prone to destroy things out of boredom.

Go-Go (also known as Silveracres Dream Catcher) started out as a search and rescue dog on the Trail Blazer K-9 Search and Rescue group. She was one of the few dogs that, when tested with cadaver scent, had no aversion to it. Because such dogs are always needed, she will specialize in forensic work. Go-Go and Lynn have been training for several months. The dogs are first taught to find people who are lost in a wilderness setting, then go on to training that focuses on the specialty in which they will work.

In order to become certified by the Federal Emergency Management Association (FEMA), the dogs must complete twelve to eighteen months of steady training. They are then considered ready for certification testing. Go-Go will be a part of their mortuary team.

When disasters strike in the United States or overseas, such highly trained dogs (who have the type of specialized instruction needed for a particular situation) are flown to the sites to aid in the rescue work.

Go-Go, a conformation dog, is working toward her championship. She also does therapy work with the disabled and elderly, and is working on her CDX.

Silveracres Dream Catcher, C.D. "Go-Go" Co-owners Lynn Godbee and Doris McGlaughlin. SAR Samoyed trained by Lynn Godbee

Photo courtesy of Lynn Godbee

Another career choice?

At 3 a.m., Alice Lombardi's Sam named Terry came to her bed, growled, then ran off. Alice rose and went to the window. She saw flashing red lights and heard a man in a tree holler "I'm not coming down until you take that beast away!"

Alice ran out the door into the yard.

"Lady, go back inside. We have a burglar!" called a policeman.

Alice saw Terry holding a large wad of cloth in her mouth.

"*You* don't have a burglar! My *dog's* got the burglar!" she answered, then called "Terry, drop the man's pants!"

Terry immediately let go the mouthful of cloth.

The officer then said "Look! That dog is smiling!"

Ch. Barchenok's Desire, July 1957, Lead dog of Alice Lombardi's sled dog team and burglar's nightmare.

Photo by Bennett courtesy of Alice Lombardi

Chapter 6

Sidelines of the Fancy: Owner Activities

Samoyed Rescue Organizations

(Information provided by Heather Schmidt)

Samoyed rescue organizations are operated solely by dedicated volunteers who rescue, rehabilitate, and place homeless dogs of this breed in permanent, loving homes. The groups rely on fund-raising and donations for support, and volunteers donate a great deal of their own time, energy, and money. All donations are spent on the rescued Sams' veterinary care.

Sometimes people cannot keep a Samoyed due to financial difficulties, a divorce, a move to an apartment, or simply because they are irresponsible. In some cases, the dog develops habits the owner cannot cope with because he or she is unaware of training methods that can correct bad behavior. Such a dog is better off in another home if one can be found. The majority of Samoyeds in shelters have been neglected or even abused.

Rescue groups locate foster homes for the dogs until permanent ones can be found. Some Sams are house-trained, but those that are not learn quickly when treated with patience and given time to feel

Heather Schmidt and friends. She founded two non-profit groups: Samoyed Rescue of South Texas and Noah's Ark Animal Sanctuary for dogs and cats condemned to euthanasia because shelters cannot find homes for them—Heather does.

secure in their new surroundings. Older dogs seem to adjust particularly well. They have outgrown some of the more undesirable puppy habits, and are always grateful for the love and attention of a stable home.

Breeds that become fashionable through movies and publicity are not infrequently exploited by greedy people. Puppy mills already abound, but will surely increase as unscrupulous individuals indiscriminately breed popular dogs. In such settings, the dogs are treated inhumanely, are inbred, and lack good care, veterinary attention, and proper socialization.

Caring people can donate money, temporarily house and care for the rescued Samoyeds, help bathe and groom them, or transport them to the vet or to their foster homes. Donating a bag of food, a spare brush or two, shampoo, a crate, or any item useful for dogs will help.

A network of cooperative rescue organizations exists in the U. S. and Canada. The phone numbers of those in or near larger cities can be obtained from veterinarians, kennel clubs, at dog shows, or possibly through Chambers of Commerce.

Here is some information is from Heather Schmidt, who founded both of the following organizations.

Samoyed Rescue of South Texas
11659 Jones Road PMB 103
Houston, Texas 77070
Website www.samoyed .com\SRST.HTM

Noah's Ark Animal Sactuary
11659 Jones Road PMB 103
Houston, Texas 77070
Website www.noahs-ark-sanctuary.org
Phone 281 469 8742

(Noah's Ark rescues dogs and cats that are about to be euthanized from shelters and finds homes for them.)

Non-Tech Photography

Dogs in general, and puppies in particular, are photogenic. Because of their antics, they can be challenging to capture on film. Do not waste time if you have one or more Samoyed pups. They grow so quickly that each day brings new possibilities and unexpected adventures as they learn to toddle about.

Sams readily make themselves available for photography with their inimitable smile and eagerness to please. Their winning appearance and willingness, coupled with their sense of humor (sometimes bizarre), provides for a wealth of marvelous shots. They are capable of making an amateur photographer look good, even when he is not even trying. All one has to do is spot and capture the moment. There will be plenty of them, all flashing by at the speed of light. Is this easier said than done? Certainly, but the effort is worth scrambling about like a mad person, oblivious to wild weather, phones ringing, police sirens, or rice boiling over on the stove.

The best way to capture your Samoyed's antics is to keep your eye glued to the viewfinder. A certain amount of athleticism and flexibility will help as you leap about, trying to keep the action in focus until the composition of the picture looks right. Scraped knees and elbows may

Astrid, owned and loved by Susan Matterling and her husband, Kevin Bohacs.

Photo courtesy of Kevin Bohacs.

come with the job. Also, be sure to get down to the pup's eye level. This is essential to avoid distorted images of his body—unless you are after some unusual effects.

If you wish to become an expert in the mechanics of photography, take some courses. Otherwise, invest in a good camera that has fully automatic functions. This will enable you to concentrate on both the action and the composition of the photo. Keeping a wary eye on things is difficult enough without trying to find the correct knobs and dials to push and twist. With a one-shot camera, you can more easily spot unsightly background objects that you do not want in your picture. Also, expect the unexpected. Not only can you can bank on it happening, it makes for some priceless shots.

Pending disasters offer wonderful possibilities—puppies pulling down a tablecloth as the china takes flight; another staggering blindly about with his head stuck in an empty box; a Sam snatching underwear out of the clothes dryer; or several puppies happily exploring the interior of a dishwasher that someone left open. A photo of a pup grabbing an ornament off a Christmas tree could become next year's greeting card. (Note: if you try the Christmas tree undecorating act, be sure to keep some extra bread handy. You can stuff the puppy with it in order to pad any swallowed shards of glass on their trip through his intestinal tract. To insure a happy holiday, make a speedy trip to your vet.)

You will learn to anticipate some spur-of-the-moment action. However, if you cannot get positioned for a shot quickly enough, relax and wait. These opportunities are like a bus. Another will be along soon. Just be ready—and patient. Also, learn to think ahead. Visualize how you want your photo to look. Balance the center of interest with a secondary object or two, such as a bush, a bucket, or a toy. This can even be done with the major subject (your dog) off-center, but balanced by a lot of space on the other side. Such efforts will result in a photo that will lead an observer's eye directly but unobtrusively to its planned focus.

You might consider enlisting the aid of a fleet-footed, quick-thinking accomplice. Such an assistant will enhance your chances of getting the action you want on film, yet avert the culmination of a disaster.

Call in a friend or conscript your spouse, stock up on film, and keep the camera handy.

You can prepare for a photo session ahead of time by filling your pockets with edible bribes or laying a trail of favorite toys. One priceless photo may cost days or weeks of effort and tons of film. Your results, however, will prove that the struggle was worth it.

Contrasting background colors and correct lighting will highlight your Samoyed—yet a white dog photographed against a white backdrop can be dramatic. When outdoors, avoid too much sun or glare. A few shadows may be needed for contrast and to create depth.

To perk up your Sam's expression just before you snap, chirp like a bird or meow like a cat. Squeak or toss a toy. You may want to station someone off camera who will assume the responsibility of making sound effects. This will also cause the dog to look away from you and your camera, avoiding redeye in your photos.

Including favorite toys, chew bones, or even partly destroyed objects in the picture will appeal to all dog owners. A photo of a puppy earnestly gnawing on a shoe or two pups tugging on a glove captures a common experience. If you cause a viewer to laugh, brush away a tear, or exclaim "I've been there!" then you and your camera—and your Samoyeds—will have achieved winning ways.

Fun With Fur

That beautiful Samoyed fur that piles up like snowdrifts in the corners of your home has other uses, believe it or not. Not only can it be knit into vests, jackets, scarves, caps, and gloves when spun, but it can also be used for more artistic endeavors, such as a needlepoint portrait.

The portrait will be most successful if the subject is a Samoyed. The example pictured here is the exquisite likeness of Don and Dot Hodges's Ch. Kipperic Sunny Peterson, BISS. This beautiful custom yarn portrait was made by Chris Lewis Brown of Toledo, Ohio.

Dog fur has been integral to at least one mystery story. The ubiquity of this substance in a canine household is wonderfully described by Susan Conant in a book from her *A Dog Lover's Mystery* series. A homicide detective is puzzling over dog hair found in the depths of a stab wound. Another character says something like "Of course it's there! We have dogs. We eat dog hair. We breathe dog hair. The mystery would be if it weren't there!"

With Sams, it's truer than it may be with other breeds.

It's there, so you might as well do something constructive with it. Here is expert spinner Sally S. Paulissen's article on unconventional uses for Samoyed fur.

Yarn portrait by Chris Lewis Brown Ch. Kipperic Sunny Peterson, BISS

Spinning With Samoyed Hair

By Sally S. Paulissen

"What are you doing?" she asked suspiciously. The woman peering at me from the door of her motor home seemed baffled as I looked back at her from my position beneath the grooming tables.

I had come to this dog show to enter my little papillon in a class, but I had ulterior motives. I'd recently learned how to spin wool and now I wanted other fibers. I wandered through the grooming area, which was set among some pine trees. So far, I had found nothing useful; poodle clippings here, bichon snips there. Then I hit paydirt. Clearly, Samoyeds had been groomed here. The reddish pine straw was dappled with tufts of white. No one was around, so I slipped out my bag and proceeded to harvest. That's when this lady surprised me.

"It's O.K.," I babbled stupidly, "I'm a spinner." I was embarrassed. My words tumbled out as I raced to explain my new hobby.

She listened impassively. Then she said, "I have more of that at home. Do you want it?"

It is interesting that many people instinctively feel that Samoyed hair should be good for something and it ought not be thrown away. Samoyeds are a natural resource for an abundant product! One feels the desire to gather and recycle this beautiful stuff from our beloved animals. Even folks who haven't yet learned about making products from the hair have been known to save pillowcases full in their closets.

Dog hair yarn sounds unusual and exotic to us. We live in a culture where people consider sheep, goats, llamas, and even rabbits as appropriate sources for fiber. But in some cultures, dogs have played a traditional role. On the west coast of Canada, for example, indigenous people of British Columbia domesticated a special variety of dog just for its importance as a fiber source. Logically, you can understand that if you lived in a climate inhospitable for grazing animals, you could not maintain sheep or goats. On the other hand, domesticated dogs could survive wherever the owners provided a meat-based diet.

Ch. Dorka of Drayalene, granddaughter of "Yurok,"
and Mrs. Wilna Coulter who is wearing a dress
featuring handwoven Samoyed fur on pockets and
skirt. Fur donated by Ch. Yurok of Whitecliff.

Courtesy of Mrs. Don Coulter (Wilna)

At spinning demonstrations, I have had people happily bury their faces in a hank of scrumptious Samoyed yarn. But when the same people were told that the yarn was from dog fiber, they reacted. Some recoiled in genuine horror or disgust. Others were incredulous but intrigued. Most were delighted.

Some of the horrified people feared that I had slain the animal to obtain the fiber. Being a vegetarian and a dog lover, that thought horrified me, too! I constantly repeat to children and adults that the dogs were unharmed and that the hair was collected during a pleasant grooming session.

Samoyeds are one of the best canine sources for spinnable fiber—maybe even the best. The abundant coat can be spun into a fine, delicate thread or plied into a luxurious, bulky yarn. A garment made from Samoyed fiber will develop a fuzzy aura, which enhances the visual effect of softness.

Many pure and mixed breeds produce spinnable fiber. How can you tell if your dog's hair will spin? Take a handful of hair from the dog's brush. Hold the clump with one hand, and with the other take the tip of the clump in your fingertips and twist it as you gently pull the fibers slowly away from the mass. If the hair will twist together into a coherent strand, then it is spinnable.

If you plan to collect your dog's hair for spinning or felting, it important to keep him clean, healthy, and free of vermin at all times. He will appreciate this, of course. After bathing and drying the dog, save the clean brushings. Discard any matted, soiled, or stained pieces. Protect the clean dry hair from mildew and moths by storing it in a pillowcase or a paper bag. These containers will thwart moths yet allow air circulation. Pillowcases should be tied shut and bags should be taped closed.

You may spin the dogs' hair directly from the dog or the brush, if you like. Spinning Samoyed straight from the dog would probably yield a woolly, textured yarn. To create something finer or with more uniformity, you would want to follow the steps most spinners would take. These steps are described below.

Once you have accumulated enough dog fiber for your purposes, you can begin making yarn. This process is identical to that of making yarn from wool, with the exception of "oiling." Sheep wool contains lanolin and grease. These heavy, sticky substances actually make the steps of carding and spinning much easier by reducing static electricity and helping the fibers cling to one another. Dog hair lacks these, so you need to add oil prior to carding.

The Spinning Process

Sorting

Make a work area by spreading an old bed sheet or paper on the floor. Brown craft paper, cut-open paper grocery bags, or blank newsprint all work well. End rolls of blank newsprint are often available free from newspaper printing facilities.

Pick through your collected hair. As you handle it, pull clumps apart, fluff the pieces, and discard any mats. You may remove guard hairs if you like. Because guard hairs are hard and slightly wire-like, they will impart that feel to your yarn. On the other hand, guard hairs can be blended in to add strength. Remove leaves, twigs, and flea bodies—anything that you do not want to be incorporated into your yarn. After sorting, your fiber should be light and airy like milkweed fluff.

Most dogs are not one color. Even radiantly white Samoyeds may have an area of cream color. Some breeds will have quite a variety of hair colors. You could work with each color individually or blend the colors together. For example, in the fur that I collected from one collie, I identified five bright colors: rust, cream, white, gray, and brown. Blended together, the result is a heathery light brown.

Oiling

This step is not done with sheep wool. What oil should you use? Frankly, it doesn't make a lot of difference. Spinners have their own preferences, but the oil is just a tool and will be washed from the yarn at the end. I have used commercial cooking spray, olive oil, canola oil, mineral oil, and baby oil with fragrance. The oil you choose can be poured into a small pump spray bottle.

Spritz the sorted hair with a little oil. Fold the mounds of hair together to blend and spritz again. You want to lightly mist the hair with oil. Do not wet the hair. Mix the hair several times then wrap it in clean paper (not printed newspaper) for thirty minutes, or overnight.

Carding

Hand cards or a drum carder straighten and align the fibers. Carding your fiber prior to spinning makes spinning easier and produces a more uniform yarn. The word comes from the Latin *cardus* (thistle). Early carding was done with a tool made from dried thistles. The long spines were perfect for straightening the fiber. Portions of carded fiber can be made into rolls or removed in batts.

Spinning

This is the fun part. Your dog hair may be spun on a drop spindle or on a spinning wheel. A spinning wheel is faster than a drop spindle; otherwise, the product is the same. You may desire singles (a single thread), or you may want the spools of singles to be twisted together (plied) into two-ply or even three-ply yarn. Directions for spinning a single ply yarn with a drop spindle follow.

Washing

The yarn is tied in a hank and washed gently to remove spinning oil and wet the yarn for setting the twist.

Setting the Twist

The wet yarn is hung under tension to dry. This will cause the yarn to hold its shape, even when dry. It will not un-spin. Drying time can take from one to three days, depending upon the weather. Once dry, it is ready to use!

Frequently Asked Questions

"If you wear a sweater of dog yarn and you get caught in the rain, do you smell like a wet dog?"

This a common question, and the answer is maybe. It depends on the condition of the fiber.

All fibers have a characteristic aroma. You will find a smell pleasant or not, depending upon your background and memory associations. Sheep wool has a peppery odor (which I find comforting); flax has a lovely hay-like fragrance; dog hair will, of course, have its own distinctive scent.

My personal evaluation of the aroma is that it reflects the animal's health, diet, and care. For example, I had two bags of Samoyed hair—two dogs, different breeders. One bag looked like white cotton candy and smelled like shampoo. The other bag also looked like cotton candy but smelled very strong and sour. Both made lovely yarn. The first had virtually no odor ever. The second batch, even after repeated washings, retained a strong smell. The odor seems to be intrinsic to the fiber structure, and is not just carried on the surface.

"If I am allergic to dogs, can I wear dog hair garments?"

Without knowing exactly what about dogs triggers your allergies, I cannot say for certain. Perhaps an allergic person would be able to wear a cap or vest of dog hair—something that does not touch the skin. If in doubt, err on the side of caution and avoid dog hair garments.

However, a person who is allergic only to the lanolin in wool could wear dog hair, because dog hair does not contain lanolin.

"What will my dog think?"

Your dog will be interested! When I have fiber and yarn in the room with my dogs, whether it is sheep wood, wolf, llama, or dog, I must defend it from the canine, feline, and avian members of the family. My son's cat liked to sleep in the fiber and tried to eat it. His cockatiels land in the basket of fiber. My dogs try to mark the fiber and steal the yarn. One comical incident (well, it's funny now) happened when one of my papillons waited for me to leave the room. She then snatched a finished ball of Samoyed yarn and ran out the doggie door with it. She dropped the ball, but the tail of the yarn caught in her collar as she continued to flee. When I returned to the room moments later, I found a trail of yarn going in and out of the dog door. The culprit was easily identified.

"What can you do with dog hair yarn?"

Anything that you can do with wool, you can do with Samoyed yarn. Weave, knit, crochet, stitch, lace, or knot. Create blankets, baskets, throws, caps, vests, scarves, mittens, shawls, or anything else that comes to mind. Imagine doing a needlepoint portrait of your dog with exactly the right color yarn! You can even make felt from the unspun fibers.

"How do you care for dog hair fabric?"

Care for your Samoyed items the way you would care for wool: gently handwash in cool or lukewarm water; do not twist or wring; dry flat. Protect it from moths. Moth larvae can damage any animal fiber.

"How much hair do I need to make something?"

One ounce of clean, spinnable fiber will yield one ounce of yarn. Fiber that is dirty weighs more because of the soil clinging to each strand of hair. Washing removes the soil and some of the weight.

Hat and scarf woven from Samoyed fur.

What do you want to make? Say you spotted a dapper cap in a knitting book. The pattern would tell you how many ounces of yarn were required. If the pattern called for six ounces of yarn, you would need to start with at least six ounces of unspun fiber.

"How do I find someone to spin this for me?"

Hmmm, well, you might consider learning how to do it yourself! Spinners are few and far between, although the hobby is alive and well. Spinning is not difficult, but it is quite time-consuming and therefore the services could be expensive.

To locate a spinner, knitter, or weaver in your area, begin by calling local yarn shops. Look in the phone book under headings such as "yarn," "spinning supply," "weaving supply," or "knitting". Ask the owners about craftspeople. Ask if there is a Weavers' and Spinners' Guild in your area.

A spinner may ask to see a small sample of your fiber to evaluate its spinnability and cleanliness. You may also ask to see a sample of his/her spinning.

"Can I learn to spin my pet's hair?"

Yes. Spinning is a simple skill accomplished with simple tools. For many millennia, men, women, and children spun yarn using drop spindles. The spinning wheel is a relatively modern invention in the history of humanity, having been around for only a millennium or so.

I found a teacher, took some lessons, and practiced. I spun wool in front of the TV late at night, or while I waited at school for my son, or while I was a passenger in a car. My drop spindle and a bag of fiber went everywhere with me. It took me two weeks to reach the "Ah-Ha!" stage. Then I felt like I understood what was happening with the fibers. You may be a quicker student!

How To Spin With a Drop Spindle

Supplies Needed: Drop Spindle
1-2 meters (1-2 yards) of genuine wool or dog yarn (not acrylic)

Samoyed Fiber

Prepare the Spindle (Illustration #1)   Tie one end of the yarn to the spindle, just above the whorl. Put a half hitch around the bottom of the spindle. To do this, make an **e** with the yarn and put the bottom of the spindle through the loop of the **e** (Illustration #1) Make another half hitch near the top of your spindle. Your yarn and hitches should look like the illustration. (Illustration #3)

You have just tied on a "leader," the first thread on the spindle. Your new fibers will cling to the fibers of the leader. Allow at least 30 cm (12 in.) of the leader to suspend the spindle.

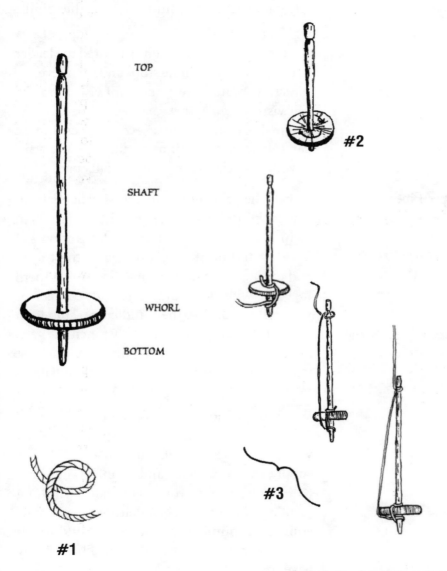

TOP

SHAFT

WHORL

BOTTOM

#1

#2

#3

Illustrations Sally Paulissen © 1994

Try the Spindle

Hold the end of the leader thread in your left hand and give the spindletop a quick twist clockwise with your right hand. (Illustration #2) You may reverse the hand instructions if you are left-handed, but you must still twist the spindle clockwise.

As it spins, notice how tightly twisted the leader becomes. As the spindle stops and then reverses direction, watch the leader untwist. Stop the untwisting when the yarn seems back to its original texture. Do this several times, but be careful: if you continue to unspin the yarn beyond its original state, it will fall apart.

Spin Fibers

To help the leader grab onto the wool fibers, open the end of the yarn a bit. Untwist the last 8 cm (3 in.) and fan out the fibers. (Illustration #4) Take a handful of your fibers. Lay the frayed end of the leader in your fiber and pinch them together with the thumb and index finger of your left hand. Give the spindletop a spin with the right hand and then quickly pinch the yarn just below your left fingers. This keeps the twist from running up into your fiber supply. (Illustration #5)

Watch the spindle slow down. Stop the spindle before it unwinds. Catching the spindle between your knees works well. Pull up on the fiber supply with your left hand, going about 8 cm (3 in.) away from your right hand, drafting (pulling out) a few fibers. Release the pinch of your right thumb and index finger and watch the twist run into your drafted fibers. They have been spun.

#4

#5

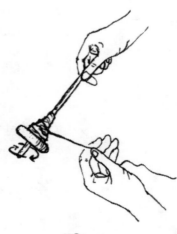

#6

Illustrations Sally Paulissen © 1994

Pinch the spun yarn with your left hand. Try not to let the twist run intentionally into your fiber supply: it would make really fat yarn and would make drafting difficult. You control where the twist stops by where you pinch the yarn. You control the thickness of the yarn by how few or how many fibers you draft.

If your yarn seems too loosely twisted, simply give the spindle another spin. On the other hand, if the yarn is too tightly spun and is trying to kink and curl, then let your spindle unwind counter-clockwise a bit.

Winding On

When you have spun a long piece of yarn and find that you have to hold your arm high to handle it, then it is time to wind the yarn onto the spindle. Let the left hand maintain its all-important pinch on the yarn to keep it from unspinning. With the right hand, undo the half hitches at the top and bottom of the spindle. Keeping tension on the yarn, wind some of the yarn onto the base of the spindle, above the whorl. Do this by rolling the shaft of the spindle between the fingers of your right hand. Roll clockwise, away from you. (Illustration #6) Make an upside-down cone shape with the yarn as you wind on. Wind most of the yarn near the whorl. Leave enough yarn unwound so that you can prepare the spindle again. Replace those half hitches and spin again.

Unwinding the Spindle

When your spindle is full or when you have finished spinning, you can wind the yarn into a ball. Place the spindle in a large jar or pot while you unwind the yarn. This way, the spindle can move about freely without becoming tangled or dirty. Or, you can ask someone to hold the spindle loosely for you while you unwind the yarn. If you will be spinning again, remember to leave a leader on the spindle.

Setting the Twist

To make your yarn completely ready for whatever creation you have in mind, you must set the twist, that is, give the newly twisted yarn a permanent! Winding directly off the spindle or unwinding a ball, wrap the yarn around something: the back of a chair, a friend's upheld hands, or a stretched coat hanger. Using store-bought yarn or string, tie the hank of yarn in four places. These ties should NOT be tight. They are just to prevent your beautiful yarn from tangling during the wetting.

Submerge the hank of yarn in a basin of cool or lukewarm water mixed with a little shampoo. Press it down to remove the air bubbles. Let it soak for thirty minutes or longer. To rinse, remove the yarn. Refill the basin with clean water and submerge, squeezing gently. Repeat this step until the rinse water runs clear. Press the dripping hank of yarn between some old towels to remove the excess water.

The yarn needs to finish drying under tension. You may lay it over a shower curtain rod and suspend a weighted hanger from the bottom. A handy weight can be made from a milk bottle partially filled with water or sand. To avoid wrinkles, remove the weight and turn the yarn a few times daily, rehanging the weight until it is dry. Once the yarn is dry, it is finished! You may choose to leave it in a hank for show and tell. If you will be using it for crocheting or knitting, you may want to ball it again.

Read More About It

Good for you! You are learning about an ancient skill. There are many, many more interesting things to learn about yarn, spinning, weaving, and other fiber arts. If you want to find out more, start at your library. Craft stores and shops that specialize in spinning and weaving sell books, supplies, and lessons. If you have a local Weaver's and Spinner's Guild, you will be blessed with help and information.

By making something beautiful and useful from our dogs, we demonstrate yet another way to enjoy and honor them. Dog yarn provides a new medium for artistic creativity. Unlike wool collected from anonymous sheep, yarn made from fibers collected from our beloved animals bears untold sentimental value. You will have a lasting treasure.

Sally S. Paulissen, copyright 1998

Selected Bibliography

Crolius, Kendall and Anne B. Montgomery. *Knitting With Dog Hair.* New York: St. Martin's Press, 1994.

Kroll, Carol. *Putting on the Dog.* Jefferson, WI: Kroll Publications, 1987. (Available from the author: Kroll Publications, W3016 Green Isle Drive, Ft.Atkinson, WI, 53538. This is my favorite book for learning about spinning dog hair. The author is an educator and a Samoyed owner.)

MacDonald, Dorothy K. Fibres, *Spindles and Spinning-Wheels.* Toronto: Royal Ontario Museum of Archaeology, 1944.

Toy Sams

Several years ago, Susan D. Amundsen, a Samoyed fancier for thirty years, decided that she could make a better stuffed toy Sam than the few commercially available. She obtained some materials and spent two years cutting patterns, assembling little Sam bodies, and then, unsatisfied, tearing them apart to try again. She did this until she reached her goal of constructing an extremely life-like replica of the white dog with the smiling face.

She now offers three different sizes of both a standing and a sitting Samoyed, all handmade from her own patterns. The eyes are authentically almond-shaped and the lips are rimmed with black leather. The open, smiling mouths reveal pink tongues ready to wash a friend's ears.

Susan Amundson holding Pistol and Hero. Mom has her mouth open.
Photos in this section courtesy of Susan Amundson

Susan started from scratch to realize her dream. She attributes her success partly to her husband, who encouraged her in this endeavor. The trade name of her creation is Bjelkiersam HERO. It incorporates the Eskimo word *Bjelkier,* meaning white breeds white, with *Sam.* Hero is the name of one of her beloved dogs. Susan is also the author of a children's book that features a Samoyed.

Yet Another Talent

When Pixie was several months old, Pat's gold harp fascinated her. At practice time she would bring her favorite toy to squeak along with the harp music. This was her own idea. They played duets until Pixie's jaws were tired. Pixie later turned to other amusements.

Pixie—pup, music lover and critic

Chapter 7

The Mechanics of the Dog Show

Dog shows are regulated by the American Kennel Club (AKC), which was established to keep an accurate register of purebred dogs; oversee activities; and educate owners, breeders, and the general public, always keeping the best interests of dogs in mind. The organization publishes an informative monthly magazine, *The AKC Gazette*. It is accompanied by a separate listing of current dog shows in the United States.

Individual kennel clubs elect a member to represent them at the AKC, so that all have an opportunity to express their wishes and ideas.

Dog shows give people a chance to learn about various breeds, which aids them in making wise decisions regarding what breed is suitable for their lifestyle. Dealers present a variety of supplies and equipment for purchase—some not readily available at pet stores. The comparison shopping at these shows is heavenly.

For the uninitiated (and those still learning), a wise buy at a show is a catalogue. It is compiled by the show superintendent and sold by the sponsoring kennel club. The catalogue lists the competing dogs, their birthdates, parents, breeders, and owners, as well as the numbers on the armbands of their handlers. It also offers more information, such as which breeds comprise the different groups, the point system (which may vary), and the rules of the show.

Judging begins with puppies, males first, then females. The pups are separated into classes by age. First a class of pups aged six to nine months is judged, then pups aged nine to twelve months. Finally, those dogs in other classes are judged. The first place winners in all classes, called "class" dogs, compete for the title of "winner's dog," as well as championship points. The females then compete in the same fashion. The male and female winners then enter the ring at the end of the line of "specials" (those dogs who already have Ch. [Champion] before their names). The latter are vying for Best of Breed (BOB). The winner is given points based upon the number of dogs in competition. The number of points is determined by the AKC, and varies from year to year as well as by area. The maximum number of points that can be accrued in any single show is five.

The specials build up points in an attempt to place as high as possible in the United States. Occasionally, to the chagrin of some exhibitors, a judge will give the BOB to one of the class dogs! If it is the best in the ring, so be it.

The BOB is chosen from each breed represented in the seven groups. Then the group judging begins. The groups, in permanent order, are Sporting, Hound, Working, Terrier, Toy, Non-Sporting, and Herding Breeds. The top four dogs in each of the seven groups are chosen. Then all seven of the "group firsts," as they are termed, enter the ring to compete for the coveted Best In Show (BIS).

Exhibitors at the shows are usually happy to answer questions, but find it difficult when standing at ringside. They are busy observing the judge's procedure before they enter the ring. Try to catch them at a more opportune moment. Professional handlers are usually racing about, juggling ring-time, grooming, and conflicts. You may want to ask them for phone numbers and call at a later date.

Although dog shows seem to be a madhouse, they are fascinating exhibitions. Observe the frantic scene with interest—and a few caveats. Do not pet strange dogs. Ask permission first. Unsupervised youngsters are not looked upon kindly, so take heed, parents.

Amateur photographers are afforded wonderful opportunities to take shots of dogs wearing sweaters, jackets, even lacy panties (on females in season). Poodles and other such breeds may wear curlers, while long-eared dogs sport snoods. Bows and fancy hairclips abound. Some dogs wear shoes while fording flooded ditches and muddy streets. The comical sights are endless. Incidentally, the owners some-times cause more amusement than the pooches.

Junior Handling

Junior showmanship competitions are held in conjunction with dog shows, both all-breed and breed specialties. The Juniors are judged only on their ability to handle their dogs—the quality of the dogs themselves is not considered.

Class divisions are:

Novice	For boys and girls at least 10 years old, but under 18
Open	For boys and girls at least 10 years old, but under 18, who have won three first place awards in the Novice class
Junior	Boys and girls at least 10 years old, but under 14
Senior	Boys and girls at least 14 years old, but under 18

Junior handlers are listed by their armband numbers in the show catalogue. The dog shown must be owned by the Junior or one of his close relatives, and must be eligible to compete in the all-breed show or obedience trials. At a specialty show, the dogs must be of that breed. For example, if the Junior handling competition is held at a Samoyed specialty, the Juniors must show Samoyeds.

Juniors are judged on "proper breed presentation, skill in the indi-vidual dog's presentation, knowledge of ring procedures, and appearance and conduct." He or she should display an "economy of motion," be quietly efficient, keep the dog's attention, show the dog to its best advantage, gait him well, and be careful to not obscure the view of the judge.

This is a wonderful activity for young people, as well a time that the entire family can share in cheering on their budding handler.

Ch. Starshine's Remington O'Pixie

  Photo by Alvin Gee

Each year at the Westminster Dog Show in Madison Square Garden, the top winning Juniors of that year compete for a grand prize which is usually something like a trip to Crufts, the prestigious British dog show.

The sight of a young person handling a mannerly, well-groomed dog in the ring is appealing. The Juniors often become quite professional, and some continue their handling careers as adults. Others make extra money and even pay their college expenses this way.

In the 1970s, eleven-year-old Lori Wendelin handled Ch. Pushka of Snowcliff (son of Ch. Sho-Off's Dorok of Whitecliff) at a show in California. The judge later said that his first thought was, "How ridiculous to send a child in the ring," but added that "she was as good as any of them!" The two made a stunning picture—the dainty little girl with the big dog she could have ridden into the ring—and electrified the spectators by winning Best In Show.

Information about this activity is available from the AKC, kennel club members, or the show superintendent (who will be located near the show ring).

Showing a "Junior" the Ropes

Three-year-old Pat, granddaughter of Agnes Mason, had been instructed NOT to cross the street in front of her house. However, the house opposite had a producing walnut tree and young Pat decided that she wanted a walnut. She crossed the road herself to get one. Her family had not missed her.

Ch. Whitecliff's Chattigan, a.k.a. Chatterbox (because of his loquacity), appeared out of nowhere, crossed the street, and grabbed Pat by the seat of her pants. He dragged her all the way back across the road into her own yard. She got the message.

Only the sheriff, who lived across the street, observed and later reported the incident.

Chapter 8

Judges and Judging

Judges are an integral part of the sport of purebred dogs. Necessary in the conformation classes, they also work in the obedience and agility rings and at flyball relays, in addition to the many other competitive activities of the sport. Their decisions strongly influence the conformation, performance, and management of dogs, and affect the future of the canine world.

Only those people who meet the stringent criteria set by the AKC will be certified to judge.

Here are some comments by several long time, highly respected judges of Samoyeds.

Judge Catherine Bell
Knoxville, Tennessee

"I have been watching the Samoyeds for twenty years and have seen a great improvement in the breed. I am glad to see that the biscuit color is not being penalized the way it was in the past, and have pointed out to others that it is in the Standard that the Samoyed Club of America approved through the AKC," stated Judge Bell.

She suggested that Samoyed breeders mentor more prospective judges. Taking the time to teach such neophytes would result in an improvement of the breed. From coast to coast, breeders and handlers shared their experience with Judge Bell at the ringside, which she found to be very helpful.

When judging, she gives each dog in the ring the same courtesy, amount of time, and thorough examination. She enjoys both judging and the dogs. "I love the Samoyed!" she exclaimed. "They have the faces of angels!"

Judge Bell is a director of the AKC Canine Health Foundation. A retired nurse anesthetist, she bred Akitas for twenty years.

Judge Frank Grover
Helotes, Texas

"When an owner-handler shows his dog, he should do so because he is proud of it. If a person radiates that attitude, it comes across subtly to the judge, possibly also affecting the major party present, the dog," says Judge Frank Grover. "Concentrate on showing the good things," he advises. "Do not try to hide anything. Let the dog do what he does best within the discipline of the occasion."

Judge Grover notes that a judge really has only two minutes to look at the dog, and must judge what he sees during that time. Thus, it is vitally important that the dog show his good points for all—especially the judge—to see.

Judge Grover judges shows both in the United States and abroad. He states that, in Australia, the judge's time is most important. Ring stewards are certified to manage the entire ring procedure, which allows the judge to focus solely on the dogs. Having no distractions makes judging faster and better. Judge Grover thinks that this system would work exceptionally well in the United States, because the extra time would allow judges to be more thorough.

Judge Grover also volunteered a bit of advice for owners on canine health. He noted that in earlier times, when working dogs performed many utilitarian duties for their owners, the length of their lives was unimportant because there were always descendants ready to replace them. Now, however, as canines fill roles as companions and service dogs, their longevity has become very important to their owners. Tiny dogs can live for up to twenty years, while the giant breeds die much earlier, with eight years generally the maximum lifespan. Dogs of intermediate size fall within these extremes. However, you can maximize your canine's chances at a long and healthy life by controlling his weight.

Your dog's weight is a critical variable in his health and lifespan. Judge Grover stated that you should maintain your Sam's weight at sixty-five pounds or less in order to keep him healthy and productive for a long time. Controlling your canine's weight will reduce stress on his organs and joints, thus allowing him to spend many happy and healthy years with you.

Judge Vera "Bunny" Hyman
Englewood, New Jersey

Judge Hyman says that "Many years ago, there were two outstanding Samoyed dogs on the show scene. I had the pleasure of putting the first point on one dog from the puppy class at his first show. He acted up and wouldn't stand still, but he was friendly, animated, and perfectly beautiful. There was no denying him. The other dog, also beautiful and correct, came under me later in his life and stood perfectly still without any animation. This made a difference to me. I gave the first dog all I could give him every time he was shown to me because he asked for it. Not only asked for it, but barked at me the whole time. I loved it! One day the second dog appeared in my group ring at a very big and prestigious show. This time he never shut his mouth no matter what the handler did. I gave him a group placing much to the surprise of the handler. Later he came to me to apologize for the dog's behavior. I told him that that was why I put him up. I loved his spirit.

When I judge this breed it first must look like a Samoyed to me. I go strictly by the Standard on what it must look like. I will most likely not even consider an 'untypey' dog in any breed. Then comes the soundness and movement. If I can find all of that, then I judge his spirit. You see, I am judging conformation, not behavior. A Samoyed should be lively, play with the handler, and have a lot to say. Then he is my choice!"

Judge Hyman has enjoyed judging Samoyeds, both in the United States and abroad. She bred and exhibited St. Bernards for thirty-five years.

Ch. Whitecliff's Alexis, age 12
  Callea Photo, Shelton, Washington, courtesy of Wilna Coulter

Judging: The Standard Described

By Don and Dot Hodges

Priorities in the Ring

We feel that judges have a tremendous responsibility to select winners wisely, because the judging process in the conformation ring has a strong impact on the future of the breed. As breeder-judges, viewing the judging process as the selection of future breeding stock influences what we believe should be emphasized and what we think can be given lesser significance.

Consider, for example, grooming, handling, and training, all of which can play a significant role in the conformation ring but are not going to translate into better puppies in the whelping box. Handling, grooming, and training have a definite impact on how a dog looks and moves in the short time the judge sees it, and no judge can completely disregard them or remove their influence. The judge's job is to evaluate the dogs in the ring as they appear, not as they might appear if…A judge cannot play the guessing game of wondering how a dog might move, appear, or behave had it been better handled, groomed, or trained. That said, as long as the handling is sufficiently good for a judge to evaluate basic conformation, as long as the dog is sufficiently trained to allow evaluation of temperament and physical conformation, and as long as the grooming does not detract from the exhibit's general appearance or coat quality, the judge should be able to reach a decision about the dog's worthiness as potential breeding stock. Further consideration of handling, grooming, or training should not, in our opinion, take precedence over the fundamental conformation of the exhibits being judged. Thus if two exhibits are presented well enough for the judge to properly evaluate their conformation, it strikes us as very inappropriate to place an inferior specimen ahead of a better one because the handler did a better job of grooming or presenting the dog that day. We believe that type of judging should be reserved for the junior showmanship ring.

Of course, much more than physical conformation and temperament play a role in breeding stock selection; pedigrees, hip and eye certifications, and other health aspects, which no judge can or should attempt to evaluate in the ring, play just as important a role in breeding, but when all is said and done, the importance of the ring evaluation cannot be overemphasized.

Judges can only select their winners from the dogs entered at a show and, as not uncommonly happens in small entries, they may find their choice limited to dogs that do not match the picture of the winner they would like to select. They must then decide which attributes are more important than others. The major breed characteristics as described by the standard and the function of the breed as a working dog provide guidelines for these circumstances. Keeping in mind that people bring to the judging process their own set of experiences and their own interpretation of the words in the standard, knowledgeable people can differ in their conclusions about which exhibits are best on a given day. The two of us, for instance, can and have disagreed on placement of a particular entry on a given day, though we agree on most aspects of the breed. That is what makes dog shows interesting, and it is often what motivates people to become judges—the belief that they have a clear

Ch. Kipperic Kandu of Suruka Orr, C.D., BIS, BISS

Owned by Don & Dot Hodges

understanding of the breed standard and can do a better job of judging the breed than others. Consider the following items, which reflect our own set of priorities when we judge the breed.

Starting with the dog as it first appears in the ring, the important points are proportion and general balance, size, substance, and coat. In other words, does the exhibit give the outline and appearance of a typical well-balanced Samoyed, not extreme in any feature?

Taking proportion and general balance first, the standard emphasizes the importance of proportion to the dog's function ("...should not be long in the back as a weak back would make him practically useless for his legitimate work, but at the same time, a close-coupled body would also place him at a great disadvantage as a draft dog. Breeders should aim for the happy medium.... Because of the depth of chest required, the legs should be moderately long. A very short-legged dog is to be deprecated..."). So the questions that the judge evaluates while generally sizing up the exhibits include whether the leg length is 55% of height at the withers, whether the dog is just off square (5% longer than tall), whether hocks are approximately 30% of hip height, whether the dog exhibits pleasing tuck up and a firm topline, how the neck blends into the shoulders and whether the neck is proper length, whether the tail seems to have proper length and set, and so forth. Balance means that visually all parts of the dog belong together (rather than looking like the work of a committee), i.e., the sum of the different parts looks like a functional whole. No one part is exaggerated or extreme. Do front and rear angulation match? The standard states that "...gait should be free, balanced and vigorous, with good reach in the forequarters and good driving power in the hindquarters..." Entering into the evaluation of balance is the relation of size and substance. A dog that has proper balance is neither too light ("racy") nor too heavy ("clumsy") for its size.

Size and substance are important defining characteristics for the breed: "If selecting a breed designed exclusively to perform draft work for a nomadic tribe, one might immediately think of a breed such as the Alaskan Malamute, which is very well designed to perform heavy draft work with great endurance, or a Siberian Husky, designed to perform lighter draft work with greater speed. The Samoyed, however, is not a single purpose dog; designed to be a "utility dog" capable of performing both herding and sledge functions, it is by necessity a compromise in construction and performance. That its functions included herding large animals over considerable territory meant the dog must be smaller, quicker and more agile than its Malamute relative, placing it closer to the Siberian Husky in this respect. The requirement that it also haul moderate loads over very long distances made it desirable to have a substantial dog."[1] While there is not a disqualification for size, the standard does say that an oversized or undersized dog should be penalized according to the extent of the deviation. We almost never see undersized dogs (less than 21 inches for a male, less than 19 inches for a female) but we do occasionally see oversized dogs (over 23.5 inches for males, over 21 inches for females), more commonly females than males.

With respect to coat, the standard makes the point that quality is more important than quantity, and in particular we believe judges and exhibitors alike can confuse good coat with long coat. A short stand-off double coat is an extremely weather resistant coat and should not be considered any less desirable than a longer coat with proper texture. We hope all judges, in evaluating coat, will not be tempted to reward the long glamorous coat that, because of its excessive length, cannot stand straight out from the body. Such coats are far less weather resistant, as the coat droops under the weight of snow.

As the judge approaches each dog in the ring for individual examination, first impressions regarding proportion, balance, size, substance, and coat quality can be confirmed or adjusted. In addition the head shape and elements that make up typical Samoyed expression (eye shape, ear set, and lip line) can be examined closely. According to the Samoyed standard, expression "…is very important and is indicated by sparkle of the eyes, animation and lighting up of the face when alert or intent on anything." These elements help to define Samoyed type and distinguish it from similar related breeds. The lip line should be close fitting and should form the Samoyed smile, which is an important breed characteristic and should be evident whether the mouth is open or closed. Ear set has a particularly important impact on the alert expression desired in the breed and helps to

Ch. Starshine's Thompson O'Pixie says "Biscuit is fine with him—and judges too."

Photo by Pat Goodrich

differentiate the Samoyed head from that of the Siberian Husky or Alaskan Malamute. Eye shape and color have a very significant impact on expression as well, so it is no surprise the standard states eyes: "should be dark for preference…dark eye rims for preference…round or protruding eyes penalized…" An overdone head may seem large and out of balance with the rest of the dog, and usually exhibits an exaggerated stop rather than the "not too abrupt, nevertheless well defined" top required by the standard, poor smile (loose flews), coarse muzzle, large round eyes (sometimes with chiseling around the eyes), and not uncommonly a rounded or domed skull rather than the wedge-shaped slightly crowned skull sought. At the other extreme, one sometimes sees heads that are snipey with weak underjaw, lack of well-defined stop, and lack of breadth to the skull, which may create the overall impression of a head that is too small and out of balance with the rest of the dog. These dogs may still exhibit good expression—good eye shape (although perhaps too closely set), ear set, and smile—unlike the overdone heads, which rarely do, but neither head type is correct for the breed. The key word we use to describe a good head is "moderate" with good expression, not an extreme head.

Closer examination also permits evaluation of feet, pasterns, and tail set, among other things. For a working breed in Arctic conditions, good feet are an essential element. Because of the multi-purpose function of the breed, the standard calls for a longer "hare foot," which

Ch. Kipperic Sunny Peterson, BISS
Owned and bred by Don & Dot Hodges

assists with speed and provides support in snow (the concept of the snow shoe), but with toes arched, not splayed, so the foot is less prone to forming snowballs between the toes. The Samoyed has a pastern that exhibits some slope and give; it is not a perfectly vertical pastern, which would not only make the dog more vulnerable to "knuckling over" but would also make him tire more easily and move less efficiently with shorter strides. None of this should be interpreted as justification of the long weak pastern we sometimes see on Samoyeds, however.

Tail carriage is an important breed-defining characteristic. While a tail carried over the back is characteristic of all Nordic breeds, the shape and placement of the tail differ from breed to breed. Too many Samoyeds in the ring today have tails carried too tightly over the back, and kinks or double hooks in the tail (a definite fault according to the standard) are not uncommon. The tail should be "mobile and loose." We are bothered greatly by judging that places great importance on seeing the tail over the back the entire time the dog is in the ring. The standard clearly states that "the judge should see the tail over the back once when judging." With that requirement satisfied, the judge can see and evaluate everything necessary. Placing such great emphasis on always keeping the tail over the back tends to reward dogs with tight tail carriages rather than the loose and mobile tail carriage required. As indicated in the standard, the tail should be "carried forward over the back or side when alert, but sometimes dropped when at rest." Do not confuse these ideas with a low tail set, which contributes to poor tail carriage for the breed (a tail carriage that looks more reminiscent of an Alaskan Malamute than a Samoyed). Short tails are also not uncommon in the ring today; the tailbone should reach the hock joint.

Watching each dog move coming and going and from the side, one can pick out those dogs that move efficiently, without unnecessary motion of the limbs or evident weakness in the pasterns or hocks. Some of these problems will have been noted on physical examination or even distant observation, but they will be confirmed when the dog moves. Side gait should be smooth and balanced, with good reach in the front and strong drive by the rear. The stride should be quick, agile, and well timed, not lumbering or plodding. We have occasionally heard breeders or judges praise dogs that are overangulated in the rear for their ground-covering gait (sometimes even their flying trot), when in fact careful observation of the side-gait reveals lack of balance in their movement—padding in front, and overreaching by the rear.[2] A quick, agile, well-timed stride is not the way we would describe this gait. We're equally baffled by statements to the effect that side-gait is more important than how the dog moves coming and going. Side gait is so interrelated with how the dog moves coming and going that we find them inseparable. They are simply different ways of drawing the same conclusions regarding the dog's efficiency in motion. True, two balanced dogs, one with proper front and rear angulation, the other with less (but balanced) front and rear angulation, may both move properly coming and going, and the differences between them will be most evident when evaluating side gait, making the choice between them clear as far as movement is concerned (to quote the standard, "A choppy or stilted gait should be penalized.") In that sense we can agree with the statement. However, a dog that does not move efficiently on the down and back (e.g., paddling, cow-hocked, weak hocked, not single-tracking, etc.) is conveying the same information that a careful observer will find when watching that dog's side gait (it translates into lack of reach or drive, overreaching, padding or pounding, etc.). Because efficiency in motion is at the heart of the breed's ability to do the work for which it is designed, its importance cannot be

Ch. Kaleis Fanya Felice,
BOB, Santa Barbara K.C.

Photo by Vicky Cook,
Fox and Cook

overemphasized. Having watched this breed in the ring for the last thirty years, we have seen its ups and downs, the fads and extremes that come and go, and considerable variability from time to time in the breed's movement. At the time of this writing, what we are seeing in the ring suggests that movement should be an even more serious concern than usual.

Special Issues for Nonbreeder Judges

There are some special issues for nonbreeder judges on which we would like to comment.

First is the issue of color. The breed standard indicates pure white, white and biscuit, cream, or all biscuit are acceptable colors. Judges new to the breed are sometimes puzzled by the term "biscuit." Biscuit can vary from a very dilute buff color to quite a deep orange-brown color. It often changes with the age of the dog, so pronounced deep biscuit coloration on extensive areas of the body is more likely in a veteran class than a puppy class. Biscuit shows up most commonly on the ears, but can just as well show up as freckles on the face, a mask around the eyes, or in patches elsewhere on the body. It can be confined to the undercoat, or color the guard hair, or both. Dogs with extensive biscuit in the guard hair typically exhibit a slightly different coat texture in those biscuit patches—an oilier harsher texture, which is extremely water repellant. Historically, the cream or biscuit Sams carried the better nose and lip pigment, so incorporating these colors into the breed standard played an important role. People newer to the breed sometimes confuse biscuit or cream coloration with stain. A Samoyed coat will stain to a creamy or biscuit looking color for a variety of reasons such as frequent contact with dirt or playful interaction with other dogs that results in saliva stain of the coat. Stain does not usually extend all the way to the base of the undercoat, so dogs with yellowish coat on the tips but white coat near the roots are more likely stained (or have a dead coat that is sunburned or about to be shed). Constant licking or tearing, or frequent contact with hard surfaces such as cement, can turn affected areas of the coat a reddish-brown color.

Second, let us reiterate for emphasis our previous comments about coat length vs. texture. Remember that length is not what it's all about; a good weather resistant coat can be short or long, as long as it has proper undercoat and good straight outer coat that stands straight off from the body. In addition, let us comment about puppy coats, since the issue sometimes raises questions for new judges. Puppy coats are often softer than adult coats, and can be charming to the eye. Puppies sometimes carry much more fuzz around the ears, making the ears appear much smaller than those of a typical adult. In our many years of breeding we have not found that good or abundant puppy coats always translate into good adult coats; indeed often there seems to be little correlation. The puppy without the fuzzy ears or unusually thick puppy coat may ultimately have just as good a coat as the puppy who does have these characteristics.

Third, let us comment on nose, lip, and eye rim pigment. The standard states that the nose should be "black for preference but brown, liver, or Dudley nose not penalized. Color of nose sometimes changes with age and weather." Living in Wisconsin, we can vouch for the latter. It was not an uncommon experience for us to find that dogs we sent to live in the South kept their wonderful black pigment to very old ages, but littermates we kept in Wisconsin often lost their black nose pigment by the time they were several years old. Some members of the

Ch. Kolinka's Quilted Bear (Hoss)

Photo by Joan Ludwig, courtesy of Joyce & Eugene Curtis

fancy, apparently unaware of the definition of Dudley, have faulted the flesh-colored noses (almost a "Rudolph the Red-Nosed Reindeer" color in cold winter weather) seen on some Samoyeds as inconsistent with the standard. "Dudley" is defined as a flesh-colored nose, which can look as pink as the skin that may be found elsewhere on the dog. The point to be made with respect to pigment is that the standard has indicated a preference for black pigment but has specifically proscribed penalizing departure from this preferred color, largely perhaps because historically the inheritance of the white coat in the breed seemed to be linked with poorer pigment. Thus, given two animals of equal quality in all other respects, pigmentation can come into play as a deciding factor in making placements. However, placing a Sam of otherwise poorer quality ahead of one of better quality on the basis of nose pigmentation alone is not acceptable, given the priorities established in the breed standard. It is not uncommon to find breaks in lip pigment as well, which in our breeding experience have no relation to pigment intensity elsewhere (dogs with intensely black eye and nose pigment, and intensely black lip pigment where the lips are pigmented, may nevertheless have pigment breaks on the lips, for example). In judging the breed, we would treat these no differently than already indicated above with respect to nose pigmentation: the standard indicates black as an item of preference, and does not indicate its absence as a serious fault. There is a fine line, however; if the absence of pigmentation on eye rims or lips is so extensive that is seriously affects expression, it should play a bigger role in the decision process than otherwise.

Fourth, back to the issue of size, it is embarrassingly common for judges who face a class containing great variation in size to assume the large dogs are the correct size and the small ones are under the standard. Nothing will upset exhibitors more than having a judge tell them their dogs were penalized for being too small when they are actually in the middle of the standard. So let us reiterate that it is so rare to see an undersize dog in the ring that this bias toward large dogs needs to be re-examined. Remember that the Siberian Husky one typically sees at a show, because it is a measurable breed with a disqualification, is usually pretty close to the size range called for by the Siberian standard. The Samoyed is not a measurable breed since the standard does not have a size disqualification, but the standard calls for the same bottom and top range for males as the Siberian Husky standard for males. If a male Sam looks as though it could fit into the range of sizes typically seen in the Siberian ring, you have a pretty good indication of proper size. If it looks as though it could compete in the Malamute ring, you know you have a considerably oversized dog. Sam females have the same bottom range as Siberian Huskies, but Siberian females may be one inch taller at the top of their standard than Samoyeds. So a Sam female that looks taller than the size typically seen in Siberian female competition is definitely over standard. Keep in mind of course that since size is not a disqualifying factor for Samoyeds, it should be considered only to the extent of deviation.

Fifth, let us comment about the breed temperament briefly as it relates to exhibiting. Samoyeds are active curious dogs who do not usually comply with demands for remaining posed like statues for significant periods, and judges who expect that kind of behavior or who penalize those who do not comply with such demands have forgotten the purpose of the show—to select Samoyeds who exhibit those characteristics typical of the breed. Because of their busy personalities, Samoyeds may not animate constantly either. Their minds wander to other things, they can become bored easily, or (in the case of males) they may zero in on the female in heat at the show or at home and forget all else; demanding nonstop animation again defeats the real goal of selecting dogs typical of the breed. Patience can be a good virtue for judges of the breed, particularly with puppies, since they may play games and act silly despite all the training the owners have invested. In line with these comments is our prior observation regarding the tail always being over the back. Dogs that relax, are hot, or bored may drop their tails. It is not only natural, it shows the tail is not so tightly carried that it cannot be dropped easily. Remember the ideal tail is loose and mobile.

A Judging Philosophy

We have all been exposed to the game exhibitors sometimes play of criticizing a winner (unless it is their own, of course) for whatever flaws the dog may possess, while ignoring the assets the winner has to offer, as a basis for attributing to a blind judge their own dog's loss. Since all dogs have flaws, this game can be played regardless of the winner selected. Unfortunately, that type of thinking sometimes pervades the judging process itself. The judge can become distracted from the process of picking the overall best dog by dwelling exclusively on shortcomings. Such fault judging, if practiced widely, would produce a breed of mediocre specimens. Returning to the viewpoint of the breeder, from our perspective the purpose of the process in the ring is to select dogs that have something to contribute to the breed in the whelping box. It is a sad day for the breed when a judge, dwelling completely on the obvious faults exhibited in the ring, selects a mediocre dog with nothing either grossly wrong or particularly right, rather than selecting the dog that might have an obvious fault but some outstanding assets as well. Which dog will contribute the most to the breed? The mediocre dog with nothing really right has nothing to contribute. The dog with some outstanding assets as well as an obvious fault has a definite contribution to make if properly mated. Faced with a group of dogs, none of which has everything we seek in the ideal, we would much rather be accused of picking a winner that, for example, has an outstanding head, structure, and movement but possesses a poor coat, or a winner that has an outstanding head, coat, and move-

Am. & Can. Ch. Kipperic Kandu of Suruka Orr, CD
Owned by Don & Dot Hodges

Photo courtesy of Don & Dot Hodges

ment but possesses legs that are on 50% rather that 55% of height, than to be accused of picking a winner we could only praise by saying "there was nothing terribly bad."

We have shown dogs for thirty years, often with one of us watching from outside the ring while the other exhibited inside the ring. That experience taught us many things, including the realization that dogs are not inanimate objects whose characteristics are unchanging and always on display to any judge taking the time to evaluate them. We have been struck repeatedly by the variability a dog can exhibit in the ring. We are not referring here just to the obvious elements such as coat condition and showmanship. Small changes in weight or conditioning can greatly affect how a dog moves. How well the dog feels, whether the dog has been on the road for long periods, and how much exercise the dog has received, can all have an impact on performance in the ring. Have you noticed how some puppies seem to move reasonably well while young, but exhibit obvious structural problems when they mature (or vice versa)? Recognizing that the dog on the end of the lead may not be showing the judge what was evident yesterday, or last week, or two years ago is important to this discussion because we as judges are charged with the duty of judging the dog as we see it on that day, not as we remember how it looked six months ago at a show (or even yesterday). It can sometimes prove difficult for a judge to forget prior performances of a dog, but in fairness to all exhibitors in the ring that day it is essential that those memories be erased. What this means, of course, is that a judge can appear inconsistent in placing a set of dogs differently one time vs. another, unless the exhibitor has watched the competition on both occasions. I remember, in particular, an occasion on which I was stewarding for a judge in the Samoyed ring. The judge, known as one who placed great emphasis on proper movement, selected as her winner an exhibit that I had seen often before. From my good vantage point near the judge, the winner, on this day, definitely did the best job of the exhibits in the ring of showing good movement, but I marveled at the fact since the dog had not shown much inclination to single track in the rear before. I later heard a disgruntled exhibitor criticize the judge for selecting a dog that could not single track—obviously this exhibitor had not watched the competition closely that day and formed an opinion from previous competition. We hope judges do not make the same mistake.

Parting Shots

Our purpose in writing this piece was not to cover all elements of judging the breed. As should be obvious to anyone familiar with the standard, there are many aspects to the breed covered by the standard on which we have not so much as commented. Many of these are obvious enough directly from the standard that we do not feel a need to elaborate, and we do not want to turn this commentary into an extensive reiteration of the standard itself. We trust that anyone truly interested in the breed will take the time to study all elements of the standard carefully.

Our intent has been to provide some guidance on major characteristics of the breed that, as breeders and judges, we feel are important breed characteristics, and to temper the trend of making the judging process simply the selection of show dogs, i.e. dogs whose major, and perhaps only, real asset is their showmanship, grooming, or presentation, which—as we have already indicated—contribute nothing in the whelping box. We hope you enjoy judging the breed, whether it is from inside the ring as a judge or exhibitor, or outside the ring as a spectator. There is much to be learned and enjoyed from the process. The greatest thrill we, as judges, experience is the enjoyment of seeing really outstanding representatives of the breed.

About the Authors

Don and Dot Hodges have been Samoyed fanciers for more than thirty years. Under the Kipperic prefix, they have owned and/or bred fifty-nine champions, numerous group winning or placing dogs, and a half dozen Best-in-Show and/or Best-in-Specialty-Show winners. They have had two National Specialty BOB winners as well as a few obedience titlists. Their canine club activities have been diverse, including specialty and all-breed club members, officers and committee members. Don has been president and AKC delegate for the Samoyed Club of America, and Dot has served as president and show chair for their local all-breed club, among many other roles. Together they have written articles for a number of publications. Don is currently approved to judge Samoyeds and Alaskan Malamutes; Dot is approved to judge Samoyeds and Siberian Huskies. Don's professional life has been spent as a biochemistry researcher at the University of Wisconsin for twenty-five years. He is now retired. Dot taught economics in the University of Wisconsin system for many years and currently serves as managing editor of a professional journal, *Econometrica*.

End Notes

1   "Samoyed Size in Relation to Function," by Don and Dot Hodges, unpublished article included in Samoyed Club of America Judges' Education Packet.

2   In McDowell Lyon's classic book, *The Dog in Action*, padding is described as bringing "into play the abductor muscles of the forearm, those that bend the elbow. These lift the leg and pad higher, suspending them in the air for a fraction longer time and then drop the pad into place." (McDowell Lyon, *The Dog in Action*, New York: Howell Book House, 1950; Sixth printing 1969, p. 139).

Doggie "Don'ts" for the Show Ring

The day Ch. Sho-Off's Czar of Whitecliff won final points to his championship, he was to return to the ring for BOB competition. The judge had draped his jacket over a nearby chair, for it was hot that day in Petaluma, California. One pocket was gaping partly open.

As Don Coulter led Czar past the chair to the ring, the dog, hardly breaking his stride, lifted his leg and, with practiced aim, filled the pocket.

Witnesses at ringside gasped. "Oh, no!" some exclaimed. The judge, busy across the ring, saw nothing.

A couple of years later the Coulters heard that the judge, Carly Harriman, had wondered about his wet pocket. Incidentally, he was former New York governor Averell Harriman's brother.

Chapter 9

America's Four Footed Soldiers

Research and writing by
Billie L. Danz and Pat Goodrich

Ancient civilizations used canine warriors. The Greeks outfitted their fighting dogs with spiked collars; the Romans trained them to attack; Frederick the Great used them to carry messages; and they were guards for Napoleon. During World War I, other countries trained thousands as sentries, sledge dogs, messengers, ammunition carriers, and casualty dogs. America had no canine soldiers of its own, but did borrow a few from Belgium and France.

Immediately after Pearl Harbor, Mrs. Milton S. Erlanger, a long-time breeder and exhibitor of dogs, had an idea. She met with Roland Kilbon, famous writer and member of the staff of the *New York Sun*. She declared that the United States must use dogs in its war effort, and reminded him that dogs had performed such service in other parts of the world for centuries. Mrs. Erlanger and Mr. Kilbon proceeded to interest others in promoting such a project. The initial group included Leonard Brumby, president of the Professional Handlers Association; Mrs. William H. Long, Jr., who was knowledgeable about obedience training; Henry Stoecker, Mrs. Erlanger's dog trainer; and Filicien Philippe, an Italian well-versed in the European use of war dogs.

Mason dog team exhibited for "Dogs in Defense" about 1942.
Far left: Aljean Mason, Center: Lloyd Van Sickle, driver. On his left in
dark suit, Alta Van Sickle

Courtesy of Sandra Flettner

Harry I. Caesar, banker, sportsman, and director of the AKC was made president of Dogs For Defense, Inc., by the group that originated and implemented the idea—and Spot marched off to war.

Dog clubs, handlers, trainers, and prominent individuals supported the effort with great enthusiasm. Editors and others who realized the appeal of dog stories gave the canine soldiers unlimited exposure in publications and broadcasts.

Over a thousand dogs were recruited each month for use by the Army, Navy, and Coast Guard, as well as by civilian guards. Breeds suitable for military service listed in the *Manual On War Dogs* included several kinds of hunters, spaniels, and retrievers; German shepherds, Doberman pinschers, Great Pyrenees, Alaskan malamutes, Samoyeds, and Siberian huskies. The last three breeds could work in deep snow and icy conditions.

"While some dogs have been given as good riddance," stated a member of Dogs For Defense, "for every gift of that kind were hundreds where the giving had cost heartaches."

Most of those recruited were trained to be attack, police, sentry, scout, messenger, or mine detector dogs. Of course, sled dogs were also needed for freighting and rescue work, and this was where the Samoyeds would shine.

Characteristics of the Samoyed enumerated in the *Manual* are the following: "strong and active, with a heavy, weather-resisting coat. He is from 18" to 22" high, weighing 40-55 pounds. His coat consists of a thick, harsh, straight outer coat, with thick soft undercoat lying close to the body. Its color is some shade of white or cream. He has snowshoe feet." Special traits listed are "strength, ability to work in a team, endurance, ability to withstand cold weather, and feet suitable for travel over snow and ice."

Training camps were established at Fort Royal, Virginia; Fort Robinson, Nebraska; Camp Rimini, Montana; San Carlos, California; Bettesville, Maryland; and Cat Island, Mississippi. Over eleven thousand dogs had been sent for training by 1943. The sledge and pack dogs trained at snowy Camp Rimini. Photographs show Sams preparing to be trained as scout dogs as well.

The training centers were flooded with letters to the new recruits from their families. They even received Christmas cards. Owners, in turn, were sent thank you letters and assured that the dogs would receive the best treatment. However, they were also told that wartime secrecy prohibited the disclosure of more information.

The men chosen to train and handle the dogs had to be of outstanding character and care deeply for their canine partners. Only the best and brightest of men and dogs would be sent overseas.

The dogs had to pass rigid tests. Their serial numbers were tattooed on them. Each dog had his own house and was provided with proper food and medical care, including shots. They were trained by the soldier who would be their permanent human partner, using overwhelmingly positive reinforcement. Part of the handler's written instructions stated that "The use of the word 'no' [should be] the only negative part of the trainer's instruction, and kind words [should be given] for reward, petting, and allowing the dog to perform his favorite exercise, including play." The manual went on to remind handlers that "every training period must conclude with petting, praise, and encouragement."

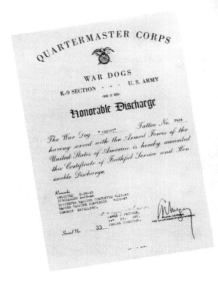

Soldier Frosty served his country for one year and received an Honorable Discharge (left).

Courtesy of Pat deBack

Orders issued to the men covered such subjects as what, when, and how to feed, how to make his canine partner's "shoes," how to administer tender loving care (TLC), and how to pet the dog. The instructions for the recruits' care certainly parallels the methods found in sensible training systems today.

Special information on feeding and care of the dogs in cold climates was also given to the handlers, which stressed the importance of having the dogs rest for thirty minutes before and after eating. Even then, the value of this respite in the prevention of canine bloat was recognized, especially for deep- and narrow-chested work dogs.

Some dogs required special equipment, such as gas and oxygen masks, camouflage, and shoes for rugged or frozen terrain. Needless to say, Sams wore their own camouflage, making them almost invisible against a backdrop of snow. For this reason, the Russians also used them for sabotage work.

Sled teams of Samoyeds did some freighting of supplies, but much of their work consisted of rescuing pilots who had crashed in areas inaccessible to motor vehicles. In some instances, dogs, handlers, and

5/29/54

Solder Frosty, returned home after receiving an Honorable Discharge from K9 Headquarter-master Corps at Camp Rimini, Helena, Montana. Shown with A. E. Mason, Frosty was used as a sled dog and trainer.

Courtesy of Sandra Flettner

sleds were transported to accident scenes by plane. Sometimes there were no landing places nearby, and teams lost valuable time getting to the wounded and freezing men.

The Army Air Corps then decided to train dogs to be dropped by parachute at the scene of a crash. Their sled, supplies, and handler would follow them. This saved precious time—and lives. A former pilot for American Airlines, Major Joseph F. Westover, supervised much of this training at Fort Nelson, British Columbia.

The four-legged parachutists belonged to the Parapups Battalion, and were said to enjoy jumping more than the men did. The dogs wore sheepskin-lined harnesses fitted somewhat like a coat. Two dogs could be dropped simultaneously with a twenty-eight-foot chute, while a twenty-four-foot chute could transport one dog safely.

Mrs. Agnes Mason, the well-respected Samoyed breeder, permitted some of her dogs to be trained to parachute. Her famous racing teams were known in Alaska as well as in the United States for their remarkable speed, stamina, and enthusiasm for challenges. Their new occupation made news. One of her dogs, "Soldier Frosty," assisted in training of others. A volunteer, he was inducted into the K-9 Section of the U.S. Army on 30 May 1943, and received an honorable discharge on 19 May 1944. His superiors rated his conduct "excellent."

The late Tom Witcher of San Francisco, a veteran of World War II, was a trainer and handler in the Army's K-9 Corps. When he was discharged, he acquired some Samoyeds of his own, having fallen in love with those he had trained at Camp Rimini. He said that the Sams learned quickly, and would attack and hold a prisoner but would not kill him.

In remote areas, the rescue dogs' remarkable feats were unpublicized due to wartime secrecy. The Samoyeds were an ideal breed for the daring exploits of rescue work. If a group had to spend the night at a rescue site in the frozen wilderness, the furry dogs' close companionship made conditions more bearable.

The dogs were wonderful company for men who were missing their families and under the constant stress of war. Having a dog assist a platoon by scouting or hauling in wounded boosted the men's morale and made them feel more secure. The lives of a surprisingly large number of men were saved by the well-trained canines.

A female Samoyed named Tuga regularly flew on combat trips with a squadron fighting against the Japanese in the Aleutians. She wore a specially designed oxygen mask. Her human companions must have considered her a good luck charm. No other information about Tuga could be found through our research. We hope that this information will reach the right party, so that more information about her contribution to the war effort can be recorded.

Samoyeds are still used as rescue and pack dogs by the Royal Canadian Mounted Police (RCMP), according to retired Officer Brian Amm, who now serves at the RCMP training center. He says that the RCMP is responsible for policing all parts of Canada that are not covered by the provincial police, including the Arctic. "In the high north, the Samoyeds used for this were spoken of as police dogs," he added. "But it isn't in a Sam's nature to be hostile like a German shepherd." Officer Amm went on to explain that the Samoyed "is unpredictable and too independent for the rigid response and discipline of a police dog." He added that the German shepherd, which is also trained for RCMP service, both does things for a specific reason and is predictable.

When an officer is stationed alone in a remote area, he is equipped with a Samoyed who serves as both a work partner and a companion. Since the clever Samoyed is in his element in the frozen North, and being a faithful and close companion is in his blood, there must be some happy Sams serving the RCMP.

Our extensive research turned up two funny stories that will close this chapter. The breed of the dogs involved is unknown, but these anecdotes are just too good to leave out.

When American soldiers arrived in the Aleutian Islands during World War II, they discovered the epitome of the word "barren." The terrain was completely devoid of any kind of foliage. Soon Colonel William O. Ericson arrived to take command, accompanied by his dog Skootch.

The enlisted men felt great sympathy for the Colonel's dog. They ordered a sprig of a tree to be flown in along with some supplies, planted it with care, and put a little fence around it. A sign was placed near the tree that read "Umnak National Forest."

Col. Arthur Kelly relates an incident from World War II in Italy in which an enemy wardog aided an American unit.

Scouting a German position on the Gothic Line between Florence and Bologna, Major Ben Butler saw an intimidating German shepherd emerge from the edge of a mine field that protected fortifications hidden by brush and terrain. He spoke to the dog in German and called him Fritz (a common dog name in Germany). The canine's hostility immediately vanished, and he accepted a snack of C-rations. His collar tag showed that he belonged to the German forces, and that his name was, indeed, Fritz.

Assuming that the dog might know his way through the maze of barbed wire and minefield, the American officer and his battalion followed Fritz, staying in single file. They were led safely through the German emplacements, undetected and intact.

Once they had navigated the minefield, Fritz stepped aside while the GIs attacked and occupied the German command post atop an adjacent mount. The Germans apparently never figured out how it happened. Danke, Fritz!

Following is a drawing of Dog Boots, courtesy of the U. S. Army Military Institute, Historical Reference Branch, Carlisle Barracks, Pennsylvania.

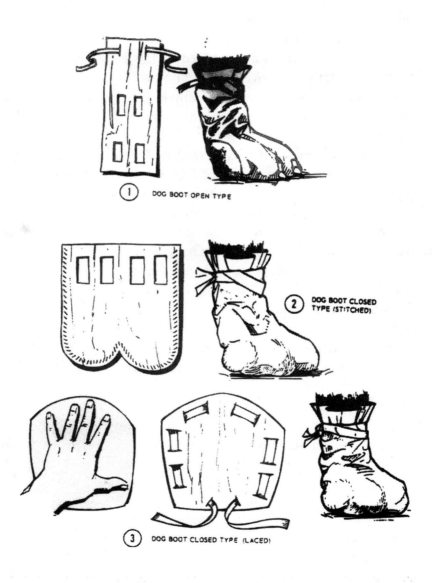

① DOG BOOT OPEN TYPE

② DOG BOOT CLOSED TYPE (STITCHED)

③ DOG BOOT CLOSED TYPE (LACED)

C-Rations?

Ch. Star Winds Kahn O'Kazakh, also known as "Wally," made a habit of gripping cans of dog food in his strong jaws. He squeezed them hard, punching holes in them with his teeth so he could suck all the food out. The cans were completely flattened when he finished with them.

Chapter 10

A Samoyed is Not For Everyone

This book is intended to better acquaint people with the Samoyed breed. White, double-coated, and plume-tailed, the Samoyed is super-intelligent, curious, and eager to do things. Of moderate size, he can participate in all sorts of activities and still claim to be his family's cuddly lap dog (weighing in at forty-five to sixty-five pounds).

If you appear in public with a sweet-faced, smiling Samoyed clad in shimmering white, be prepared to gather an admiring crowd full of questions. Plan to be off your schedule. Your glamorous canine companion will wait, patiently and expectantly, to have his ears or chin scratched.

This is an opportune moment to spread caution. Despite the fact that he is a stunning showstopper, a Samoyed is not for everyone.

If his needs and desires are not understood and heeded, he will make you aware of his misery through actions and speech. Bright and willful, the Samoyed can destroy your house, clothing, and favorite collectibles, uproot your shrubbery, and drive you up a wall.

When considering a lively, adorable bundle of fur masquerading as an innocent puppy, one must realize that the little furball needs a large space with high fence and securely locked gate, proper food, timely shots, almost daily grooming, and careful tending. You will come to think that he has ten-foot-long arms and suction cups on his feet. You must be prepared for emergencies. Write the phone numbers of your veterinarian and local poison control center on the wall, and keep gas in the car.

Sams prefer all-day companionship. Almost constant supervision would be ideal, but is probably impossible. Never leave him outdoors alone for a number of reasons, the most important being the possibility of theft. Remember, his appearance alone attracts attention.

Unless eating or sleeping, he will require something to do. This is a working breed. If he has nothing to do, he will think up activities of his own. Sams tend to be escape artists, bursting with ingenious getaway plans.

Remember, the purpose of this book is not to encourage anyone to get a Samoyed, not to motivate the opening of more puppy mills, not to promote backyard cash flow canine operations, and not to crowd animal shelters with dogs people decide they do not want after all.

If you do not have time to love and laugh, do not get a Samoyed.

However, should you fail to heed this warning and succumb to a Sam pup's charms, you must strive to understand him and respond to his needs and demands. Sure, you can put on an act about being the alpha dog in the pack, and he will allow you to think that you are. He is so clever at feigning innocence and manipulating humans that you will not catch on. If you do, it is best to keep him ignorant of the fact.

By the time the puppy agrees to a desirable routine in his new home, his humans will be trained to furnish him the life style that he craves. They will never figure out how it happened.

But they will be ruined forever for any other breed. Consider yourself warned.

Aiming to Please

Runamuck, Desi, and sisters learned during their whelping box days to "potty" on a towel in a corner. One day when they were four or five weeks old, all four dogs were entertaining a roomful of company in the living room. One of the boys had a sudden urge to "potty," but did not want to leave the good time with the guests. He rushed across the dining room and ran down a long hall to a bathroom, where he found a bright red facecloth on the floor. He dragged it back to the living room with great difficulty, his puppy legs almost inadequate to the task. All conversation ceased when he returned, dropped the facecloth on the carpet, and proceeded to potty before the hushed crowd. In his excitement he missed most of the face-cloth, but received much praise for being such a good boy.

Hoping to escape soon—into the big world. It took 3 days to get this photo—somebody always fell off the crush bar before I could snap the photo—but persistance paid off. Shortly after they became known as the "Demolition Squad."

(Left to right) D'sign'r Duck, Runamuck Duck, Adoraduk, Luvaduk

Chapter 11

Selecting A New Family Member

So you still want a Sam puppy? Read on to make yourself aware of what's really involved in taking care of that adorable furball. If you decide to progress to ownership, swear that you will never neglect it or let it see the inside of an animal shelter or puppy mill. Should you decide to breed your Sam, you must protect its descendants as well.

When you bring such a clever creatures into your homes, you must be prepared. Here are some tips born of experience.

Research   Question several breeders whose judgment you can trust. Note whether their advice is consistent. Attend dog shows and read books on the breed. Ask owners for information, and visit with them and their dogs, if possible. The AKC distributes information at dog shows, and/or you can write for booklets and a video on Samoyeds. Contact information is included in the Appendix.

Observe   Once you select a breeder, visit him or her so you can see the parents of the available puppy. Observe closely the facilities and type of care. A Sam pup who is brought up in a kennel that does not provide opportunities for socialization can be a problem and heartache.

Those first few weeks and months are most important. The mother and pups should have had reasonable interaction with their human family. The puppies need to become accustomed to household noises, adjust to a regular schedule, and enjoy loving care in a healthy and protected atmosphere. Incidentally, a pup less than eight weeks of age is too young to be taken from his mom and siblings. He needs to learn, from his mother, how to get along with others. Cutting that time short can result in behavioral problems later.

OFA, CERF, and Pedigrees Ask to see the pup's parents' certifications of healthy eyes and hips. Ask for pedigrees, as well. The latter should show which of the pup's ancestors have been certified by the Orthopedic Foundation For Animals, Inc. (OFA) and the Canine Eye Registration Foundation (CERF). Avoid purchasing a pup if only his parents show this important information. Do question the breeder, however. The initials may have been forgotten or omitted accidentally. But do insist on a complete pedigree.

The breeder may allow you to see your puppy before it is old enough to move in with you. If so, comply with his directions on hygiene. The pup's shots are far from complete. Do not be surprised if you have to wash your hands and your shoes are sprayed with a Clorox solution. You may not be allowed to touch him, either. Remember, though, these precautions are all for the puppy's protection.

Ch. Ka Leis Fanya Felice with grandson Magnum caught in mid-jump.

Photo by Pat Goodrich

Get Ready

Plan for your pup's homecoming. Children in your family will particularly enjoy helping preparing for the new arrival. Your breeder will give you instructions and suggestions. Be sure to follow them, particularly those regarding feeding. As he grows, make the necessary changes.

Preventing Disease

Mix one part Clorox and twenty parts water in a spray bottle. Now it is your turn to spray the soles of other people's shoes—or ask visitors to remove their shoes entirely. Until your pup has had all his shots, it is better that he has no company.

You should not attend dog shows yourself to avoid carrying disease home with you. Parvovirus is transmitted through the air, and it is deadly to pups. When you've been out, change your clothes and shoes in the garage. This sounds extreme, but taking such precautions will pay off. You can relax after the puppy's last shots in his first series take effect. Your friends should understand.

Quiet Time

Get your puppy when household noises are normal rather than around a holiday, when strangers will come over and want to hold the newcomer. Everyone will have a hard time keeping their hands off your adorable fuzzball. Because he is a baby, he will tire quickly. Do not allow even your children to handle and play with him incessantly. Or, rather, especially your children. This is a perfect time to teach consideration for, and kindness to, animals. Also, be sure to have your children keep their voices down, if only for the puppy's sake.

His Own Space

Your puppy needs his own space that is near the family, yet secure, quiet, and protected. This brings us to the use of a crate.

A crate is the ideal personal space for your puppy. This is the time to let him know that his crate is the greatest thing on the planet. Never, never use it as punishment. This needs to be his secure spot, where nothing can disturb or injure him. Start out with a crate that is large enough for an adult Samoyed (one that will not mash down his ears when he is grown and sits up in it). Leave the door open most of the time so he can enter and exit as the spirit moves him. Put his food in it. A stand for his dish will fit in there when he is taller and his pasterns need the room. Place his toys and chew bones in it. He might like a comfy

Pixie after her toy bear (8 weeks old)
Photo by Pat Goodrich

pad—or he might decide to eat it. The latter is extremely possible, so remove the pad immediately if he starts to gnaw on it.

When left alone at home, shut him in the crate with a safe chew bone and lots of praise. Say the same thing each time—something along the lines of "I have to leave now, but I will be back!" If he is safe in his crate, he will be unable to shred the drapes or kill himself eating foreign matter. You are supposed to have everything up high, but you will miss one thing and he will head straight for it, if on the loose.

Do not travel with your Sam until all his shots have taken effect. If and when you do at a later date, the crate will be a lifesaver. Fold it up, take it along, and set it up in your hotel room. Cover it partially with a sheet (for privacy and to avoid drafts), put him in it, and close the door. It is his home away from home, and he will feel happy and secure in the knowledge that you will be back.

If you leave your Sam alone in a hotel this way, put a "Do Not Disturb" sign on the doorknob. That way, he will not be panicked by strangers coming in. You can put locks on the crate to prevent his being stolen, but someone could carry out the crate with the dog in it, so leaving him alone is unwise.

An aside—when you travel, take along a supply of his usual drinking water. It will help him avoid bowel upsets. But just in case, carry along whatever your veterinarian prescribes for such problems as well. Remember, the watchwords of the Samoyed owner are "Be Prepared!"

Stockpile Bread

Your pup should sleep in the crate at night for his own protection. If not, he will be up to mischief, which could include swallowing things that will not go through him, or eating things that will poison him. Do not let him have the run of the house without close supervision. (Again, if you cannot do that, do not get a Samoyed.) He may chew through lamp cords, or break dishes and eat the sharp shards. Rest assured that no matter how much thought and care you put into puppy-proofing your home, he will conjure up ideas that you would never think of or believe. A previous paragraph already stressed this point, but reading it twice won't hurt. This is not to scare you, but to prevent misery for both of you.

In the event that he finds and eats something harmful that you missed, you can stuff him with several slices of bread to pad it and push it through his plumbing, or you can make him vomit. One method may be preferred over another, depending on what he ate, so be sure to call your veterinarian for expert advice.

Choosing Toys and Bones

Be careful what sort of toys you give your Sam. Even as a puppy, his teeth and jaws are in fine working order, and he has no judgment about what not to eat. He will squeak a toy for hours, but he will also open it up eventually and eat the squeaker. Watch him and remove it at the critical time. If you give him rawhide bones, snatch them away when he has a smaller piece he is able to carry in his mouth like a cigar. He is liable to aspirate it (inhale it into his lungs). Avoid giving him hoofs. Hard and sharp, they can kill. Even at six weeks of age (before you got him), his baby jaws were able to hold a tennis ball. Get him a larger ball dyed with non-fading colors that has a tough, unchewable surface—but not so hard that it will harm his teeth. Dogs have suffocated when a ball, caught at an odd angle, has lodged in the jaws. This has happened with the owner standing by, helpless.

When selecting toys, it may be wise to avoid those made overseas. You have no way of knowing whether the stuffing or any other part of the toy contains harmful material, nor how well the item will stand up to fierce chewing. Watch toys carefully, and throw them away when they become too worn for safety.

Observe

Keep a close eye on your pup, too. Know how he looks when well. A dull, glazed expression in eyes is easier to spot if you are familiar with the how they appear when he is healthy. The same applies to the feel of his fur, nose, and body, and even the way he walks. Pay attention to what he says. He will communicate with you in his baby way. Always keep your veterinarian's phone number handy. Write it on the wall or enter it into the speed-dial feature of every phone you own. Your

Pixie says goodbye to the boys.

Photo by Pat Goodrich

puppy should be acquainted with the good doctor, since you stopped at the vet's office on the way home for a check-up and an appointment for his next shots—didn't you?

Positivity

Always be pleasant, gentle, kind, and positive with your pup. Praise him lavishly for good behavior rather than punishing for bad. Remove negativity from your repertoire.

Potty Training

If he potties in the hallway, do not scold him. You just failed to get him out at the right time. Pups do not have the bladder capacity of an adult dog. Always take him out to potty right after a meal, and in-between, too. Do this very frequently at first. Later, as his bladder grows and he catches on to the system, you can relax more. Again, always pet and praise profusely when he gets it right. Tell him he is the most wonderful doggie in the world. He will be proud of himself and try to merit

I saw it first!

Photo by Pat Goodrich

more such praise. (You can laugh at him behind his back when he tries to lift a leg and spray something, but falls over. It takes a while to learn how to stand on three legs!)

Sams Are Not Subservient

In general, Samoyeds truly want to please you, and are bright and quick to learn. However, if what you demand does not make sense, you may have some explaining to do! These dogs (and pups) do not like to be treated in a subservient manner. Owners of other breeds may not understand this.

Some native groups in northern climes who used different breeds of work dogs tended to treat them as just that—work animals. The Samoyede people, as you now know, treated their dogs as partners and companions. Those ancestral genes continue to affect the modern Samoyed. This is why this breed is unhappy without something to do, and becomes distraught if not allowed to live closely with its family. It is imperative that owners understand this heritage. They are different. Sams are not subservient; however, they are intelligent, cooperative, loving, and protective. Who could ask for anything more?

Samoyeds like to be clean, and wash themselves as cats do. They will go to a corner of the yard, or away from their indoor play space to potty. They do not want to soil just anywhere. Give them a chance. Another lucky quirk of the Samoyed is that they, like poodles, have no doggy odor.

A doggy door may work for potty purposes if you are away during the day. However, if left to go outside, he can both get into more mischief—and be seen. To be seen may mean to be stolen. Do not take any chances.

However, to properly potty-train a puppy with the least trouble (if no one is home during the day), leave your job to go home at noon or at break time. You may also trust a neighbor or other good friend to help. Change your job hours, if possible, so someone will be home part of the time. Change jobs. Or do not get a pup until your schedule changes. Please be fair to him.

Puppy-Proofing

Put harmful substances and objects out of reach. Keep trash off the floor. Put away (up high) paper clips, hairpins, rubber bands, and twist ties. Watch out for nails and screws, electrical cords, and items that a pup can pull down on his head. Turn the handles of pots and pans to the inside of the cooktop. As your curious pup grows taller, he will be able to reach more. Protect the laces on your shoes. Protect your shoes. Keep all medications up high and out of his reach. Your puppy will remind you of anything you've forgotten—if he doesn't eat all the clues.

Training the Family

Teach the rest of the family to follow your example of leaving nothing within the reach of your adventurous Sam. Some pups specialize in pulling off buttons and eating them; others shred towels; yet others take nailbrushes. Brace yourself and learn to laugh a lot.

Hey! Might taste good!
Photo by Pat Goodrich

Food

Maintain an exact feeding schedule. Make your puppy rest a bit both before and after a meal. Lengthen that time when he is older to help prevent bloat. Measure his food precisely, according to his age and weight. Follow the directions on the package, or those of your veterinarian. Take time to read the contents of a number of brands of dog food. Some all-encompassing phrases may disguise some shocking inclusions, such as chicken feathers, feet, and bills. Give your dog nothing that you would not eat yourself. Dogs have died from being fed cheap food full of ground peanut shells. What goes inside your Sam is important.

A daily vitamin pill, plus a balanced diet, should be sufficient for your pup's growth and well being. Cottage cheese (a teaspoon daily) and a peeled, chopped, hard-cooked egg (several a week) are good supplements. Again, confer with your veterinarian and consult reputable books.

Do not overdo the calcium. A correct diet will furnish the right amount. A combination of hard food mixed with a small amount of water, a slice of commercially available meat roll (lamb or beef), and puppy bones or doggy bagels constitute a good basic diet. The non-fat bagels keep tartar from building up on his teeth and give him the chewing exercise he craves.

It is easy to let your dog become overweight, and those extra pounds are not good for his joints and pasterns. If you cannot feel his spine, he may be too fat. Reducing his weight will be difficult. Do not leave food out. Put leftovers away promptly. Keep fresh water available all the time.

Judicious bribery (rewards) helps. Later you can reduce the size of the treat to a crumb and your pup or adult dog will be happy, because the attention is most important to him. An occasional raisin, slice of apple, banana, carrot, or half a grape will be welcomed. (A whole grape is easier for your dog to choke on.) Avoid sweets, and allow no chocolate, which can be deadly. Canines cannot metabolize the caffeine-like compound, theobromine, in chocolate. Keep cookies and other treats up high—the odor is tantalizing to a dog.

Grooming

Start early getting your puppy used to being brushed. This should be a pleasant time, so do it gently, without pulling. Pay special attention to the fine, cottony puppy fur around the ears that becomes knotted easier than other areas. Daily brushing prevents such tangles. If one does develop, spread a pair of long, slim scissors wide apart, then place a finger behind the knot. Gently work the point of one blade through the knot, breaking it up into little strips that can be worked out painlessly. Placing your finger behind the knot insures that the blade will not go into the puppy's skin if it slips—it will only go against your finger. Do this slowly and gently. Take a break from the detangling while you brush him somewhere else, then return and continue the process until the knot is gone.

Puppies need to DIG! Tarahill's B'Dazzle O'Sunshine at 9 weeks.

Photo by Pat Goodrich

Because the Sam has a stand-off coat, brush him from his tail toward his head. Spraying his fur lightly with water first will prevent hair breakage. The proper way to brush his double coat is called line brushing. Here's how: hold the brush in one hand, using the other hand to part the fur in small sections so that you can see the skin. Brush from the skin out. You will need a regular size pin brush for his sides, back, and neck, and smaller ones for his face and ears. A small soft bristle brush is particularly good for the ears. A steel comb is useful as well, but be careful that it does not pull the fur. Both brush and comb work well on the tail. A rake is another good addition to your grooming tools. It is particularly useful when your Sam is shedding, because it catches and removes the fine hairs of the undercoat easily. Just comb it through small areas of fur from head to tail. Be very gentle and talk to your Sam while grooming him, even when he is an adult, to make the experience fun for him.

At the same time you begin grooming, get your Sam used to having his teeth brushed several times a week. However, when he is teething he is miserable enough. Forget the brushing then. (One ear may come back down at this time, but will probably go up again. Consult your vet if there are any problems.) Trimming his toenails with clippers or a grinder should be started early, too. When you hear nails clicking on the floor, it's time to trim! If they are allowed to grow too long, his feet can be thrown out of position.

Should your Samoyed have the bad luck to encounter a skunk, here is Sheila Herrmann's formula for removing the odor: make a creamy paste of about half hydrogen peroxide and half baking soda. Apply it to the yellow skunk spots. Let it set for about five minutes, then wash out with Dawn brand dishwashing detergent. Afterwards, apply a good coat conditioner several times.

Poisons

Be aware that a dog picks up bacteria and other harmful substances through the pads of his feet. It is important to consider carefully the types of cleaners you use to scrub or mop the floors he walks on. Some types of soap, anti-bacterial liquids, and other substances can be

Tarahill's B'Dazzle O'Sunshine, 9 weeks. A typical pup growing faster on one end!

Photo by Pat Goodrich

harmful. Poisons in powder or liquid form (such as insecticides) can seriously hurt or kill your dog. Exercise great caution when planning to use such products. A dilute solution of bleach in water (like the one you use in your spray bottle) is safest for mopping floors. Yet another reason to keep your dog safely in your own yard is that you probably don't know what sorts of substances your neighbors are applying to their lawns or gardens. Keep rat poison, your own medications (including aspirin and acetaminophen), and especially antifreeze out of your dog's reach.

The subject of gardens brings to mind another caution. All poisonous plants should be removed from the puppy's yard. Not only will he enjoy ripping your plants out of the ground with those big feet, but he will also (probably) taste them first.

Training

By now, you have surely been training your puppy without trying. You call him to come eat; you say "Let's go potty;" you tell him good-bye when you leave, always saying "I'll be back;" you say "No!" or "Hey, come back here!" when he runs off with your shoe. You probably say "Let's go" at the door. Start giving hand signals at the same time.

The two most important things to teach him are "Puppy, come!" and "Puppy, stay back." First, be sure to do this where there are no distractions. To teach "Puppy come," put a six-foot-long leash on him, then walk backwards so it is stretched between the two of you, lying on the floor. Gently tug a bit as you say "Puppy, come!" Keep trying patiently until he does, then hug and praise, and pull out a small treat for him. A crumb is enough. Practice for about five minutes, several times a day. Do not scold him if he doesn't come sometimes—just keep trying. A Sam learns quickly. He should graduate to coming to you off the leash, as well. This command could save his life.

For "Puppy stay back," go to a door that opens onto a porch or breezeway. Let him follow you, then step out quickly, holding up your hands in a "stop" gesture while saying "Puppy, stay back." Again, praise him lavishly and give a reward when he gets it. He needs to learn this

Aimee Phantom de Mardi Gras, "Buck", 10 months Bred and owned by Gerard and Marion Langlois

command. You can relax a bit when he responds consistently, but be alert and ready to stop him. If a squirrel, car, or other object comes into view unexpectedly, he may forget his training and rush out into a potentially dangerous area. So do not trust him completely on this; always follow through to be sure that he complies. Consistency is the watchword.

If he rides in the car with you, put him out of the way of any airbags. Children, small people, and dogs can and have been killed by them. When you step out of your car, keep him from jumping out ahead of you. Say "Wait!" and help him out after you have exited. Of course, he is always safer riding in a crate rather than loose in the car. Position it so he won't get too much sun, and so he can look out at the world flashing past. Never leave him in a closed car. Fatal heat stroke can occur in less than ten minutes. He could also be stolen in a split second. Don't take any chances.

A hallway is the ideal place to practice walking on a leash. Put some treats in one pocket, slip a tennis ball in another, and put his soft slip collar and four-foot lead on him. Say the same thing each time, with enthusiasm. It could be "Now we are going to practice!"

Have him stand on your left side. Keep the lead rather loose and say "Let's go!" in your most animated tone. Give him a little tug to get him started. If he is reluctant, hold a treat just a bit in front of him, and start walking. He should have his eye on whatever you offer, and follow you to get it. When he takes a few steps, stop and praise him, then present the treat. Repeat. This is the carrot and stick process, without the stick. Keep the lesson no longer than five minutes. Do not tire him or let him become bored. The treats will help.

Now, it is important to end a training session with a fun surprise, so take out that ball! Say something goofy like "Looky what I have!" and throw it for him to chase. You can encourage him to bring it back so you can throw it again, but do not make a case of it at this point. He has had his lesson. Of course, he may surprise you and return it himself. Reserve this particular ball for post-practice play. Make it special.

Several five-minute sessions a day are better than one that is fifteen minutes long. He will love this time with you, and will enjoy learning. He should be taught these things early. You may want to take him to a puppy kindergarten, but do not place him in a regular obedience class for quite a while yet. Wait until his attention span becomes longer. Do not risk burning him out.

Take him for short walks if you like, but do not let him do any actual road work or jogging long distances with you until he is about two years old. This may place too much stress on his bones and joints. A Sam matures slowly, and should not do a lot of jumping as a young pup. Even a leap off the sofa could injure his legs and feet when he is small and bones are soft. Help him up and down, and let him increase his exercise at his own rate.

As your Sam grows, continue the regular schedule of feeding, shots, and check-ups. Reassure him when he worries. Talk to him all the time, even if you are only explaining what you are doing.

Keep moving things higher. Remember that when he goes through his gangly stage, he can reach more. He already knows where everything is!

Thompson of the Seven Samurai

Photo by Pat Goodrich

General Care

Many ladies claim their Sams swallow some of their personal flimsies. Some panties are made of a lightweight nylon material that, charged with static electricity when fresh out of the dryer, makes them stick to other items briefly. Then they drop off on the floor when the clothes are carried off to be folded. Your Samoyed will discover these before you do. He will pad silently behind you on the way to your dryer, just watching for the opportune moment to grab a pair. This author's underwear has a high disappearance rate for the same reason. I try to be alert in order to thwart potential thieves, but they outwit me at times.

Swallowing panty hose is dangerous to those Sams addicted to stealing from the clothes dryer. This stunt can prove fatal. Again, be alert and be prepared.

Avoid Fright

If a thunderstorm frightens your Sam, try this successful solution contributed by Carol Brown.

When the thunder and lightning start, Carol gets out the popcorn, while her Sam, Laska, observes closely. Carol tosses popped kernels in the air, one at a time. Distracted by this game of catch played with edible tidbits, Laska forgets about the tumult outside. Any other indoor activity that a dog enjoys should work the same magic.

If you walk your Sam in a park, at a show, or other places where he will see strange dogs, do not let him get close to them. Be sure to avoid black or brown dogs. The sight of a white dog may cause them to feel threatened, and they may growl, snap, or want to fight. Watch out for dogs on stretch-type leads—they can leap out suddenly. Try to avoid any frightening situations; however, some will probably occur that you can't do anything about.

Bad Habits

If your Samoyed picks up a bad habit, figure out how to change your routine. For example, if he insists on pushing out of a certain door ahead of you, have him practice going out correctly (after you) at a different door for a while. Then return to the problem door, and practice there.

If he wants to take *you* for a walk, remember that pulling is in his genes; however, you can stop it. Turn suddenly in another direction. When he pulls again, go another way. Keep him off guard, wondering which way you will go next. He will start to watch your feet and follow you. Give the same command each time, such as "Stay with me!" Praise him lavishly when he gets it right. Be consistent. He will smile because he wants to please you.

If your dog has a habit of consuming foreign matter, such as paper, rubber bands, or paper clips—you name it, he'll gobble it down—get in the habit of tossing out such things.

When you bring in groceries, immediately remove and throw away twist ties or other types of closures on bags of produce. You may not notice them falling onto the floor. He will learn quickly that, when you come in with packages, he has another opportunity to pick up exciting trash. Be alert and develop your own good habits. They will prevent the illness, or even death, of your Sam.

Treats

When giving him a bit of cheese (keep it small—it's fattening!), he will watch your every move intensely. Once you cut the cheese off the block, return it to the refrigerator before giving him his treat. This will send the important message that what is cut off is all anyone will get. If you leave the block out, your Sammy will con you into cutting off some more. Betcha. Also, if you insist on giving him a bite from your dinner table, wait until you are done with the meal. If you don't, he will pester you throughout. Keep it to a morsel.

Always remember that the Samoyed wants to please his family. Praise him lavishly when he does something correctly, and tell him that he is the greatest doggie in the world. You think he won't understand? Ha! Do what is best for him, and he will pay you back with intense loyalty and undying affection.

No Place Like Home

When Pixie's litter of seven boys strongly insisted on abandoning their litter box at around three weeks, the box needed to be dismantled and put up out of the way. Not understanding the pups might be affected, Bill and Pat were taking it apart when the boys huddled together and began to wail. Seeing their cozy home disappear, although they no longer used it, not even to sleep in, really did upset them. They were hugged and comforted until they no longer cried, but Pat and Bill vowed they would take down the box out of the sight of any future litters.

All seven of Pixie's litter incarcerated in the kitchen: The Seven Samurai

Chapter 12

Your Litter

So you've decided to go the old-fashioned route—your girl has been bred and puppies are on the way! You will mark each day on the calendar while the lady-in-waiting begins to look like she swallowed a watermelon. Of course, you'll worry about whether she will have an easy time of it—especially if this is her first litter.

Prior to Whelping

Taking her to a specialist for an ultrasound examination about a week before the projected delivery date is a wise move. If all is normal when you see the little beating hearts (a thrill in itself), you can relax somewhat. If not, preparations can be made in advance to deal with any difficulties that may arise.

Expect her to start rummaging through your closets about a week before the event. She is searching for a quiet nesting place in a remote corner. She will probably prefer a deep hole dug under the porch or back steps that is out of sight and inaccessible. If given the opportunity, she may dig one—so be forewarned.

The whelping should be a joint effort among you, your dog, and your veterinarian (even if he or she is not in attendance at the actual event). Have your vet give you exact directions on how and when to start taking and recording her temperature. Counting a certain

One of the Seven Samurai escaping from the whelping box.

Photo by Pat Goodrich

number of hours forward from the time her temperature begins to drop will give you a rough idea of when you can expect her labor to begin.

A few weeks before the event, prepare a whelping box. It should be about four and a half by five feet, with sides about fifteen inches high. A drop-down door on one side will help the mother go in and out without jumping. Crush bars measuring one by three inches, placed about four inches above the floor of the box, are needed to keep the pups from being pushed against the wall by the mom. Place old sheets and blankets in it to make a clean, soft bed. Then place it in a dark, partly hidden place, maybe half covered with a sheet. Old newspapers are good to put under the sheets for padding and absorbency (keep the newsprint off the fur, or you will have a dark gray Sam). Recognize that all the bedding will need to be discarded afterwards. Should the prospective mother find all this satisfactory, she might prefer it to a hole under the porch—or your crowded closets.

Collect old but clean sheets to take to the veterinarian's office, if you hope that is where the event will occur. You will also need a box lined with blanket scraps for carrying the puppies back home.

Pack a bag with other necessities, such as a baby scale, colored ribbons for marking each puppy after it is born, and a small notebook for recording weights and color-coding. The ultrasound told you how many to expect. The ribbons will soon come off, so keep matching nail polish nearby so you can put a spot of color the size of a quarter at the base of each tiny tail. They will all look alike, so keep each pup marked and identifiable. Be sure to replenish the color as needed—it will wear off quickly as they become active. You may also want to get a syringe that can be used to give liquid medication. This is particularly useful to have on hand as the pups get older.

After the Birth

Once the puppies are born (or brought home) and comfortable in their whelping box, the room temperature must be kept even. Allow no disturbances—the mother needs rest, peace, and quiet. Keep an eye on the pups to be sure that all are nursing sufficiently and keeping warm. The mother should resume her regular feeding schedule, and keep plenty of fresh water available just outside the box.

Keep that sheet or blanket over half or more of the box. It will keep out drafts and make her surroundings dark and private—which the mother dog prefers at this time. A special waterproof heating pad for the pups, set at low constant temperature, insures that they will keep

An important visit to the vet: Aimee Samoyeds with Marion and Gerard (far right)

Pixie and her babies, the seven boys only several days old.

Photo by Pat Goodrich

warm if they wander away from the mom. Be sure that none of the puppies get chilled. For the first several nights, you should sleep nearby to be sure that all goes well. A few days of bleary, bloodshot eyes are a small price to pay for healthy puppies.

When they are three days old, take them to your vet for removal of their dewclaws. If done this early, the operation involves just a simple snip of skin and a quick touch of the cautery or a stitch (if needed). Even a few extra days' growth will make removal more difficult. Carry them to the office with a towel over their box. This will provide some protection from airborne germs. You might want to sit with mama dog in your car so she will not be disturbed by the little wails. Taking the dewclaws off is best for the pups. They can get torn loose, become infected, or become snagged on things. They end up being nothing but trouble. By the way, the Samoyed standard says they should be removed.

In three or four days, their little noses and toes will start getting smutty as the pigment genes kick in. They will squirm about, trying to crawl, and seem to grow right before your eyes. Between meals, they will stay close to their mother, draped over her paws or snuggled up in the fluff of her tail.

Socialization

Begin socializing your puppies almost from day one. At first, this should be done by you alone. Be sure your hands are clean, and don't handle the pups excessively. Hold each puppy on its back, turn him in all directions, pat him gently, and rub his tiny ears. This will get them used to being handled. Do this several times a day, talking softly to them all the while. Brush each a bit, very gently, with a small bristle brush. When the pups get older, set one at a time on the grooming table. Use extreme caution when doing this—don't let a pup fall off the table. If phone rings, take him with you. Never tie a pup on the table or take your eyes off him.

They will soon start dragging themselves around on their chubby little tummies, then begin to pull themselves up and wobble about. You now have a box full of toddlers. In no time their eyes and ears will open, and they will begin to explore the whelping box. Their little tails come up around this time, too. They will discover the private sanctuary under the crush bars where they can stretch out to sleep. When they become too hefty to squeeze under the bars, they will pull and tug to do so, protesting loudly. If there is a tiny pup in the bunch, it will

Asleep under the crush bar...   *Photo by Pat Goodrich*

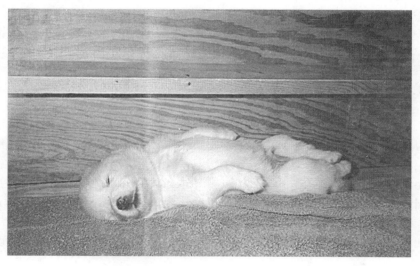

First one to sit up and howl.   *Photo by Pat Goodrich*

continue to enjoy its snoozing privacy while the others struggle in vain to find as comfortable a retreat.

Do keep your camera ready, as well as a large supply of film. Take a photograph of the mob with their mom on their first day. Then continue to record the priceless moments of their puppyhood that you will always treasure. A video camera can catch the action as they begin to swing on each other's ears, pull tails, and roll around on their patient mother.

Northern breeds, like the Samoyed, begin eating and running about early—probably because they would soon freeze in their natural habitat.

Housebreaking

When a pup leaves a puddle three inches in diameter on the heating pad, be glad that it's waterproof. When other pups begin to follow suit, you know it's time to place an extra folded towel in one corner of the whelping box. Set them on it at strategic times. At about three weeks of age, they will start eating some soupy gruel. They will also walk in it and grind it into each other's fur. A special dish will stop that, if you can find one. It has a high center and resembles a hubcap that fell off an alien vehicle. It works extremely well, though.

Immediately after they eat, set them all quickly on the towel and say "Potty! It's time to potty!" If you continue this routine, you will be surprised how quickly they catch on. This is a most important thing you can do for them. You want them to be used to being clean. Do not let them remain dirty. Keep clean sheets and towels near the box, and change them often. The new mother will wash the pups diligently— and clean up the box if you don't. She should not have to do the latter, and she needs your help with the housekeeping duties. Keep their box and play space clean at all times.

Good "reach" on this spoon thief   *Photo by Pat Goodrich*

Mrs. Agnes Mason's puppies   *Courtesy of Pat deBack*

Safety

The pups will soon learn to climb up on the crush bars and peep over the edge of the box. Long before you suspect it is going to happen, you will find one daredevil who will lean out enough to fall overboard. Puppy-proof the room they are in. Be sure they have something that will give then secure footing, such as a slightly rough towel. This is especially important when their little bones are soft.

Do not leave them unsupervised for long periods of time. They can quickly develop bad habits that will be difficult to break. Such neglect will also affect their personalities. More aggressive pups can torment shyer ones, causing them to retreat into a shell. Such behavior should be discouraged.

Keep up with their shots. Take your notebook that lists their color codes, and check off each name as that pup gets his shot. Because they all look alike, it is easy to give one puppy two shots and miss another completely. To complicate matters, the pups will be jumping about, bursting with their usual energy. You and your veterinarian will need to work out a foolproof system. This sounds simple, but it is not.

As mentioned in the previous chapter, toys must be safe. Nylabone types of toys that are small enough for their jaws but too big to swallow are fairly safe. Again, keep a close eye on toys and destroy any that are becoming worn to the point of being unsafe.

By now you are making headway teaching them to go on a leash and to "potty" in the proper place—preferably outdoors. Add the "Puppy come" and Puppy stay back" commands, and you will make each puppy's adjustment to his new home much easier for him and his new family. This early training is essential. Remember, frequent short sessions given with patience and consistency will make—and keep—learning fun.

The puppies need to stay with their mothers and siblings until they are eight weeks old at least. They learn a lot simply frisking around with each other. Their mother, in her own way, teaches them manners. They learn by observing her—and you, too.

Placing Puppies

Before they were born, you might have been keeping a list of people with good homes who are waiting for a pup. Breeding your dog is a big responsibility, but placing the pups with responsible owners is a bigger one. You and your family are attached to them, and will grieve when they leave. This is easier, however, when you are certain that they are going to the best of homes.

How do you set about placing the puppies? Ask potential owners lots of questions. Have they had a Samoyed before? If so, for how long? What happened to it? Where did they get the dog—from a breeder or a pet shop? Which breeder? Do they live in an apartment? Do they have a fenced yard? Do they want a show puppy or a pet? Do they have another dog? What breed is it? Do they have other pets? Or children? If so, what are their ages? Does everyone in the household work, or is someone at home all day? You will come up with more, but you will often be able to determine if a potential home will be good with a few questions.

Write out a contract. Put in it an agreement that if the buyer-to-be becomes unable to keep the puppy at any time, even after it is an adult, you (the seller) will get it back. Include the price and any other pertinent information. Be sure to add that the buyer is to take the puppy immediately to his own veterinarian for a checkup. Include with the contract all records of shots, eye examinations, any other health information, and pedigrees of the parents that list OFA and CERF certifications. Promise that if your pup develops hip dysplasia within a certain time, the buyer will receive another at no extra cost. Give the new owner the proper AKC forms for changing the record of ownership.

Give the buyer a separate list that spells out the feeding schedule, any medications or vitamin pills the puppy takes, and other pertinent information. Assure the buyer that you are always available for advice, and that you want to keep in touch. Explain the rest of the shot schedule, as well as the wisdom of getting the puppy tattooed (once all his shots have been given) and having regular veterinary exams.

Puppies need space to run. Here is "The Demolition Squad": Runamuck Duck, D'Signer Duck, Luvaduck, and Adoraduk.

Photo by Pat Goodrich

Pups on crush bar—almost out!

Naming the Pups

An interesting and fun aspect of having your own litter is that you get to name them. Before they are born, scribble down your ideas. The AKC limits the number of letters that may be used in a name to twenty-five, which discourages expansiveness but stimulates creativity.

The AKC requires you to have a kennel name, even if your kennel is your house. If you choose that first, it may influence your choice of names. You may want to use part of the puppies' parents' names. If father belongs to someone else, get the owner's permission before using any part of that name. Do not use it for your pup's descendants. It belongs to the male's owners.

Some breeders go down the alphabet when choosing names, while others choose a theme. Here are two examples: Ch. Ka Leis Fanya Felice had a lively litter of four sired by Ch. Kazakh's Lucky Duck. For pedigree identification, the two boys and two girls were given names including the words "Duck" and "Fanya." The names finally chosen were Starshine's Luvaduck O'Fanya, Starshines's Adoraduk of Fanya (no room for a *c* in that one), Starshine's D'sign'r Duck O'Fanya, and

Starshine's Runamuckduck O'Fanya. The group was nicknamed "The Demolition Squad" and "Little Angels With Muddy Faces."

A seven-male litter was called the "Seven Samurai," and the names of American-made guns were used as a theme. The group was given the names Remington, Winchester, Thompson, Smith, Wesson, Colt .45, and Magnum (who weighed two ounces more at birth than the other six). These names were prefaced with "Starshine's" and ended with "O'Pixie."

Remember that names you choose will remain in your heart after the puppies are gone, when you recall your cherished memories of the furry infants you were privileged to have for a short time.

All Dressed Up...

Fanya and her ten siblings, at eight weeks of age, caught on quickly when the time came for them to go to their permanent homes. When the first pup was bathed and brushed, then disappeared, the others thought nothing about it. When the same thing happened again, the remaining pups took notice. When preparations were being made for the third puppy, they ran away and hid. The same behavior occurred each time another was spiffed up to leave.

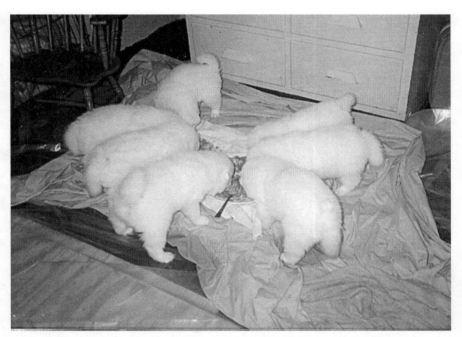

The Seven Samurai (all boys), Pixie's litter about three weeks old.

Photo by Pat Goodrich

Chapter 13

Decisions, Decisions

Have a show dog, you think? Want to give showing a whirl? You can always quit if you decide against the idea.

Is your dog of show quality? Get opinions from knowledgeable breeders, handlers, and judges. Read. Attend shows. Compare the answers you are getting. Be objective, and listen to constructive critiques from those you trust (you may want to steer clear of immediate competitors!). Do you have "kennel blindness" that assures you if it is yours, it is perfect?

■ **Would your dog enjoy it?**

Was he happy in conformation, obedience classes, and puppy matches? Take him to some if he hasn't been exposed yet. He'll let you know. If his answer is "no," don't push it. Maybe he'll change his mind later, maybe not.

■ **Do you have the time and money?**

Classes, matches, and shows take lots of both. Make lists and a budget.

■ **Will your spouse and/or family agree?**

Will they want to participate, maybe? If not, can you leave them without upsetting your household entirely?

■ **Can you be a good sport and not be distraught over losses?**

You leave yourself open to disappointments when you show your dog. Can you deal with not winning all the time?

■ **Will you become obsessed?**

Will you be "dog show" all the time and neglect everything else? Or will you be able to be reasonable and have another life? Remember, all things in moderation.

■ **Do you plan to be an owner/handler?**

Do you feel comfortable in the ring? As George Alston points out, this is the only sport where amateurs compete on the same footing with professionals. There are many pros and cons to this system, but you will be able to learn about the sport and enjoy it. Is this worth it to you?

■ **Would you prefer a professional handler?**

Observe the pros at work, then get advice from owners who use one. When interviewing a professional handler, ask lots of questions and go over every possible scenario with him or her. It will cost you money. However, the most important concern of all (as always) is whether your dog will be safe and happy.

■ **Do you want your dog to travel to shows?**

Are you willing to have him to leave home for long periods of time? Or would you prefer to take him, all spiffed up, to the ring each time to meet your professional handler?

Think this through carefully. Your dog's happiness, and maybe his life, depends on your decisions. Do what is best for both of you, and your family as well.

Top-notch mentors and knowledgeable judges are valuable sources of advice. If you decide to show your dog bear in mind that you'll win some, and you'll lose some. Just do it for fun—and think of the good friends you'll make!

The "Mad" Hatter

Always taking good care of his toys, Thompson loved his possessions. He likes wearing his little Western-style straw hat around the house. One day some visitors, unaware of Thompson's attachment to it, removed it and placed it on the head of a poodle pal. Although normally calm and laid-back, he pitched a fit about sharing his beloved chapeau. When it was quickly returned, Thompson was happy again.

Chapter 14

Puppy Matches

If you decide to show your puppy, locate a conformation class that will introduce him to ring procedure. Again, do not place him in classes until all his shots have taken effect. Ask your vet for that information. Particularly important is the Bordatella immunization, which prevents kennel cough. This illness resembles distemper, is as hard on adult dogs as it is on pups, and runs rampant at dog shows. About four months of age is a good time to start.

Find a knowledgeable teacher with a gentle hand who is pleasant, uses a positive approach, and is meticulous with details. He or she should have a special sympathy for shy puppies.

Since you plan to show your pup after he attends some conformation classes, try him first in a puppy match. Only ribbons are given out, and no points are accrued toward championships. The competition is not as serious, and people tend to be friendly and helpful to novices. A puppy match is, however, a rehearsal for a real show. This experience will expose him (and you) to the joys and perils of what lies ahead. Do be aware that what happens to him the first few times he is exposed to the procedures of matches will affect him for the rest of his show career.

This can be a grand time. The matches are designed to be informal, and can be fun for the entire family. Make a day of it, camping and picnicking on the show site, which is often a park or convention grounds.

Remember, your most important job is to be certain that your Sam's experience is a pleasant one. This responsibility starts with planning ahead, so you aren't frazzled when you arrive at the match. Carry along your own food and, of course, treats for the puppy. Take your own water for him, along with something he can drink it from. Water from a different source may cause intestinal upsets. Take his crate along so he will feel more secure in this strange place. The odd sounds made by a multitude of uneasy puppies are new to him. Throw that sheet over part of the crate to give him a bit of privacy and shield him from drafts. Bring along his grooming supplies and table, as well as several folding chairs for you and friends. Let him get used to being groomed in odd places teeming with strange dogs and people.

When you arrive at the match, mist his feet and legs with flea spray. This may keep other dogs' fleas off from hopping on him. Also, watch where he steps. There may be bits of broken glass and other trash underfoot. Remember, too, to look out for those extensible leads that may allow other dogs to get close to him without warning. This is particularly important at shows.

Walk in slowly, giving him time to look around. Pet and reassure him. Do not allow other dogs to approach the two of you—stay away from the crowds and barking pups. You will hear more barking than you do at a regular show, because all the attendees are new at this game.

Talk to him all the time, explaining things to him in a quiet voice. Praise him for the smallest thing he does right. Keep the situation light.

Your Sam will enter the match happily, but probably a bit shyly, at first. Most judges are lenient and forgiving with puppies. Generally, apprentice judges work at the puppy matches, so they are learning, too. During examination of each puppy, the fledgling judge should treat him with special care, handling him gently and giving him time to get used to a stranger feeling his body. Be alert for anything less, and take up for your pup if things do not seem right. Be sure that he is not uncomfortable around strangers. At the end of the show, when he is more relaxed, you might let a few friendly people pet him gently.

Take along your spray bottle of dilute Clorox and spray his feet before putting him in the car to go home. It is easy for a dog to pick up all kinds of illness-causing bacteria at shows through the pads of his feet.

Take every precaution possible and carry along everything you need, then relax so you and your puppy can have a great time. If he enjoys this experience, he will look forward to the next match. Then, at his first real show, he will strut his stuff like an experienced show dog. So will you. Strut, that is.

Herding...Puppies?

When Fanya and Pixie observed the author trying to catch one of the Seven Samurai puppies that were speeding about the large dog patch, the two would get on each side of the little fellow and hustle him straight to me. They knew the names of each pup, too: Remington, Winchester, Thompson, Smith, Wesson, Colt .45 (Cody), and Magnum.

Chapter 15

The Show Samoyed

With luck you may acquire a puppy of show quality through breeding or purchase. Bring him up as you would any pup, with good food, proper care, exercise, and the puppy training discussed earlier. Be sure that he gets used to varied sights and sounds, as well as other people. Help him to have a good time, and protect him from frightening experiences.

Your aim is to produce a calm, well-adjusted pup who is good-natured and curious, but not fearful. Influences in your home will certainly affect his outlook. Provide a stable atmosphere that is happy and secure. Puppies—and people too—will not thrive in unpleasant surroundings.

When his shots are completed and have taken effect, begin to take him out in public. This is great socialization for him, as well as practice for the ring. Take him to the fringes of a mall first; don't thrust him into crowds early on. He needs time to observe and discover what is going on around him, and he cannot do that if he is frightened. Take him with you to gas up the car or pick up fast food. Be aware that the latter may get him into a bad habit, because he will want a taste. Admirers at the window may hand him a tidbit if you don't! Remember that he is an adorable fuzzball, and already practicing how to get what he wants. Take him along anywhere he is allowed.

Conformation Classes

At four months of age, start your Sam in a good conformation class. Again, be sure that the instructor uses positive, not negative, reinforcement in training. Take along a bottle of water and something for him to drink it from. An understanding teacher will give puppies a quick rest at mid-session for a potty break and drink.

Your pup will benefit from a good conformation class, and both of you will profit from the learning experiences gained at puppy matches. These experiences will help you feel more at ease at your first show. You have been practicing for the real thing for quite some time.

First Show

This is an exciting adventure, but, as you did for the puppy matches, prepare ahead and stay calm. His leash is like an electric cord that conducts your excitement to him. He does not need to carry your reactions as well as his, so force yourself to be calm for his sake. Try to treat the experience as you did the relaxed, informal matches.

You will probably be in the ring first with the six- to nine-month-old puppies. Get your numbered armband from the ring steward, and wear it so the numbers can easily be seen. Step into ring when called, and follow the judge's instructions closely. You may be told to go around the ring first, then stop to set your puppy up—stack him—so the judge can examine him closely. Run your hand down his back briefly to reassure him, then, with the leash rolled in your left hand, hold his collar with the same hand to steady his head. If he tends to back away from a stranger, this may prevent it.

Again, most judges are forgiving with puppies and do not approach them from above, which can make any dog shrink back. As he or she moves down your Sam's body, keep still and do nothing to interfere. Keep yourself in the background, do not speak unless spoken to, and do not try to catch the judge's eye. A judge has only a very limited time to see your pup up close, and needs to concentrate on what he or she is

One of the Greatest Movers of All Time—Ch. Kazakh's Lucky Duck winning again at the prestigious Westminster Show. Does he have even one foot on the ground? He's flying!

Photo by Michele Permutter, courtesy of Flo, Saul, and Sue Waldman

doing. If you get a heavy-handed judge, do not subject your pup to him or her again. Treatment that is not gentle can put your puppy off shows for good.

You will have a lot to remember and do quickly and correctly. This can be daunting, but practice makes it easier. Attending shows regularly is great practice in itself, but be careful that you do not overdo it. Your Sam must be eager, attentive, and animated in the ring. Let him have a good time. Wake him up outside while you wait your turn, but play with him in the ring when judge is not looking. Remember, this is a party!

Carefully observing others in the ring (including professional handlers) can be like taking lessons yourself. Watch how they handle situations, what they do when the judge is busy with other dogs, how they get ready for the judge, and how they stack their dogs quickly on entering the ring. Even where they seem to want to go in the line-up will tell you something.

Watch the judges' routines. Try to make sense of the patterns they use, as well as why they choose certain dogs. If a judge makes him- or herself available, ask questions of them, as well.

Have a towel for your pup to rest on at ringside while you are observing, or have someone else watch him. Do not leave him alone or tire him out. Dogs are stolen at shows; if he gets over-tired, he can get sick; and too much of the show routine can cause him to decide that he's not having fun.

Another most important caveat: take along small treats to bait him with in the ring. These will keep him lively and focused on you. Give him more tidbits when he comes out of the ring, along with lots of hugs and praise. Let him choose a toy to take home. Dealers put them at dog's-eye-level for a reason. This is always fun to watch.

Your puppy has been trained to show like a champ and enjoy every minute. Don't let him chew on any ribbons he wins—they may fade, and you need to preserve them.

Show Grooming

Bathe your Sam a day or two before the show. Brush him as usual after he is dry. Groom him carefully at home, then go over him again at the show, fluffing up what got flattened on the way. You've remembered your table, grooming arm, crate, tack box of supplies, a rubber-backed mat so your dog has secure footing on the table, and Band-Aids. The Band-Aids are for you. If you are late and in a hurry, you may punch a hole in your hand with the pin brushes, and you don't want your blood getting on this white dog. Put your name on your belongings, and keep your expensive scissors, brushes, and other items back in the tack box. Unfortunately, people do steal such things. Ladies, if car is safe, lock your purse in it. You can also put items in the crate and padlock it.

Ch. Starshine's Remington O'Pixie of the Seven Samurai, age 5

Photo by Alvin Gee

Buy a bottle of good no-rinse cleaner. A light blue formula will make your Sam's coat sparkle. When you get to the show, wash his feet and lower part of legs. He will get dingy just walking into the building. Then spot clean any other grungy areas and complete the grooming. If he wiggles when you neaten up his feet or brush his tail, this may be easier to do at the show because he will be distracted by watching what's going on around him. You need to budget time for these extras, of course.

Be discreet if you use starch on your Sam's coat. It seems to give a nice finish, provided that you're not wearing black. However, if the judge finds any left in the coat, you will be invited out of the ring—a most embarrassing situation. Also, if others are grooming dark-coated dogs near you, they will not appreciate starch blowing their way.

Be considerate and polite at shows. Keep your area neat, and have plastic bags handy for any accidents. Only slobs don't clean up after their dogs. You will see a few of those.

Dress to highlight your Sam in the ring. Black is fine, but it will show fur (and starch) clinging to it. If you choose to wear it, take along an adhesive lint roller. Sueded silk does not seem to hold fur, so try clothing made of that material. A Samoyed looks fine against anything but white. Avoid white shoes, too, as judges cannot get a clear look at your Sam's feet.

The magnificent Ch. Yurok of Whitecliff (1955-1970)
Owned by Mr. & Mrs. Percy Matheron, Mrs. Jean Blank (pictured)
Bred by Mary Breatchel

Courtesy of Wilna Coultern

Women should consider wearing comfortable, solid-colored clothing that does not restrict movement (you will have to run). Do not
wear clothes that will show things you'd rather not when bending over.
If you choose to wear a skirt, be sure that it will not billow around in
the dog's path or block the judge's view of him when gaiting. Comfortable, low-heeled, non-skid shoes are essential. For men, suits or sport
jackets with trousers in colors that will provide a suitable background
for the dog are good.

There are numerous excellent books available that discuss showing
and handling your dog. Some are written by top professional handlers,
who share their expertise in detail. Read as many as you can to gain a
wider picture of the intricacies involved in this sport.

When your Sam captures the winner's bitch or winner's dog award, it will participate in the final class, that for BOB. In that case, let him rest, then groom him again just before the working group is shown, which is later in the afternoon.

Although this is exciting (sometimes an outstanding untitled dog will be given the BOB over older dogs who already have their championships), it is also a time when complications can set in. Your Sam is in the ring longer, so let him rest and relax when the judge's back is turned. Being in the ring a second time on the same day is especially tiring for a young one. The ring is much larger, so you two must cover more ground when gaiting. There will probably be more applause, which may unnerve him. There may be more professional handlers in the group ring as well. But don't let any of this rattle your nerves. Focus on your Sam and his performance, and stay calm for him. Later, ask friends who were at ringside for suggestions and constructive criticism, provided that you trust their judgment (and they know more than you do).

Show experience, reading informative books and articles, and observing the experts will help you feel more at ease in the ring and actually enjoy it. So will your Sam. Refresher classes in conformation are always an excellent idea—unless you are good enough to turn pro.

The Annual National Samoyed Specialty

Each year, the Samoyed Club of America holds its annual National Specialty in a different area of the United States.

During these exciting five or six days, the usual classes held at a dog show are interspersed with activities involving the many and varied tasks this breed is capable of undertaking. Herding, sledding, and weight pulling exhibitions may be available for aptitude/instinct testing or competition.

Sometimes, there are opportunities available for agility trials and/or obedience testing. A costume contest, a parade of champions and one of rescued Samoyeds, and a Junior Showmanship competition add to the festivities. Pack hikes are arranged, and dogs can be tested for their Therapy Dog and Canine Good Citizen titles. Usually, there is a judges' education seminar.

There is also an auction of breed-specific items such as figurines, clothing, and scarves made of the beautiful fur spun into yarn, rare prints, and other unusual objects. The funds collected help defray the

Ch. Kazakh's Wennisercio
O'Sno Dawn
"A Thoughtful Winnie"

Courtesy of Diane Sorrentino,
Owner

costs of the regular publication of the SCA's critically acclaimed *Bulletin*, as well as the operating costs of the organization (which has a membership of eleven to twelve hundred). Donations are also made to groups doing research for the betterment of the breed.

With luncheons, parties, and a closing banquet, members enjoy seeing old friends and making new ones with their beloved Sams at their sides.

Hors D'Oeuvre, Monsieur?

Lucky Duck, a multiyear Westminster winner, could occasionally be the temperamental star in charge. His handlers always brought a large selection of treats for his approval. Frequently, just about at ring time, he refused the "bait" that was supposed to insure his paying proper attention at show time.

Onlookers were amused to see the handlers scurry off in all directions in search of different goodies. One thing his handler could be sure of: the loquacious Lucky Duck would have plenty to say. However, most judges did not object to his speaking to them.

Ch. Kazakh's Lucky Duck greets the judge.

Courtesy of Saul & Flo Waldman

Chapter 16

The Kazakh Samoyed

By Florence and Saul Waldman

L ots of people have asked us: how do you breed—and show—a top-winning, multiple Best in Show dog?

Our answer? You need just two things: smart breeding and good luck. Which is more important? Well, it depends on whom you ask—and maybe whether they've done it themselves. Guess which ones will say smarts, and which will say luck.

What do we think? Both are necessary, so how can you say one is more important than the other? For example:

- We've had carefully researched breedings that were disasters, yet done others that made us look clairvoyant—with less care.

- We've sold dogs that grew up beautifully, but kept others that, well, made really nice pets.

- We inadvertently ended up with a top handler for Lucky Duck, but he was a terrier handler, so our Samoyed went to the shows that had the best judges for terriers.

- We never missed a breeding for nearly fifteen years. We were always blessed with perfect timing and participants—on both sides—who always delivered. Then we hit a wall and our bitches weren't breeding—each for a different reason. What if that had happened two or three generations earlier?

All this is to say that in dogs, as in all other aspects of life, some actions produce the intended consequences, some get mixed results, and some yield totally unintended—and even unwanted—consequences. So while good planning increases the chances of good results, there are no guarantees. Sometimes, yes, you have to be lucky.

Yet, looking back, we can identify a few principles that guided our own experience, contributed to our success, and taught us some lessons along the way. Among them:

- Deal with people you feel you can trust who demonstrate that they'll advise you on what's best for you rather than what's best for them. For example, in our early days, when we needed advice the most, Joan and John Scovin—active breeders at the time—referred us to another breeder for our first show puppy, when other breeders in that same situation might have tried to keep the business for themselves.

Ch. Kazakh's Lucky Duck, Best of Breed, 1989, 1990, 1991 (group 4)
Courtesy of Flo & Saul Waldman

Ch. Tarahill's Everybody Duck, Best of Breed, 1992, 1994
Courtesy of Flo & Saul Waldman

■ Decide which qualities make up your ideal dog and, recognizing that you will never achieve that perfection, try to determine—from observation and from pedigrees—which dogs seem to have been most influential in producing those qualities in the past and appear most likely to do so in the future. And don't ignore the bitches; or, it takes two to tango; or, the sire isn't the only producer.

In our case, we decided early on that a bitch named Ch. Whitecliff's Polar Dawn was not only incredibly good, but also incredibly influential in passing along her good qualities. So our pedigree, by design, is laced with Dawn throughout. She was the mother of Sam O'Khans and the grandmother of the Kubla Khans, the North Stars, the Weathervanes—all of which went into our early pedigrees—and of our own Kazakhs on both sides. Such was her influence on and significance to the breed.

Ch. Shada's Silver C's Just Ducky, Best of Breed, 1996
Courtesy of Flo & Saul Waldman

A few hints on breeding

■ Don't in-breed, but do line-breed. This is the best way to maintain and improve on the good qualities you already have.

■ It takes a long time to build the pedigree that you want, but just one wrong breeding to blow it. In other words, while it's correct to outcross in order to import qualities you think you need or want, take care that you don't also bring in a bad quality or two—even medical problems—with them. It's not a good trade-off when you consider that it may take generations to breed it out—if you're lucky.

■ Don't ignore temperament. Much in the way that breeders who show may believe that all their puppies are show quality, and much as they want to place them all in show homes, many—if not most—puppies bred for show will end up as family pets. They will serve well in that capacity, too.

■ And finally, have another life. Even the most fortunate among us have many more disappointments than triumphs. If we didn't have other interests in our lives, we'd go crazy—and because the dogs used up all of our money, we'd be unable to afford the psychiatric help we'd so desperately need to make us normal again.

About the Authors

Florence and Saul Waldman bought their first Samoyed in 1968 and their first show Samoyed in 1969. Since then, they have bred several dozen champions, group placers, and specialty winners over a twenty-five-year period, reaching the pinnacle of success with the 1984 birth of Ch. Kazakh's Lucky Duck. He was the number-one Samoyed in the United States in 1988 and 1989. He accumulated more than forty Group 1 wins, more than a hundred Group placements overall, and seven all-breed Best in Show wins. He won BOB at the Westminster Kennel Club show in 1989 and 1990, then retired. He did, however, come out of retirement for Westminster 1991 and won his third straight Westminster BOB, as well as a Group 4. He is the only Samoyed to have accomplished this feat. He was also a successful therapy dog.

Lucky Duck was bred to Ch. Ka Leis Fanya Felice, and has sired numerous top winners through the fourth and fifth generation. His son and grandson followed in his footsteps by winning BOB at Westminster three of the next four years. Together, these three extraordinary dogs dominated six of seven consecutive years.

Lucky Duck still lives with Flo and Saul's daughter in Arlington, Virginia.

Shake?

When Lucky Duck offers you a paw, you are obliged to take it and squeeze his toes gently. He will squeeze back. With a smile, of course.

Chapter 17

Ocular Abnormalities

By M. K. Herrmann

The anatomy of the canine eye, going from front to back, consists of the cornea; a fluid-filled anterior chamber; the iris, which is the colored portion of the eye; the lens; the vitreous cavity; the retina; and the optic nerve. The retina has the capacity to turn light impulses into electrical impulses. These are then sent, via the optic nerve, to the brain. This is how we see. The iris works like a diaphragm that controls the amount of light that enters the eye. The pupil is the opening in the iris. Visual problems can arise from any of these anatomical structures.

Samoyeds may have the following abnormalities of the eye:

Distichiasis   This term refers to eyelashes that are abnormally located at the margin of the eyelid, and usually means a second row of lashes. This abnormality may cause tearing and some corneal irritation, but is usually mild and does not cause any problems. If it is a problem, surgical removal may be necessary. These dogs can be bred, but if the breeder notices an increasing incidence and severity of this condition in puppies, then they should be left out of the breeding program.

Corneal dystrophy	This is a non-inflammatory opacity (cloudiness) of the normally clear cornea. The term dystrophy implies an inherited condition. Treatment is rarely needed for this problem.
Uveodermatologic syndrome	This condition is an immune-mediated syndrome, meaning that the body is turning against itself. It affects the eyes in several ways, all of which have the potential to cause blindness. It is usually accompanied by a depigmentation of the nose, eyelids, and lips. This syndrome can be treated with steroids and other immunosuppressive drugs. A dog with this disease should not be bred.
Glaucoma	This condition causes elevated pressure inside the eye that, if sustained, leads to blindness. It can be caused by a congenital malformation in the eye called goniodysgenesis. Unfortunately, checking for this defect is not a part of the routine CERF examination. The condition can be treated with medication, but sometimes surgery is needed to decrease the pressure in the eye. Dogs with glaucoma or severe goniodysgenesis should not be bred.
Cataract	This refers to an opacity of the lens. It can affect anything from a small part of the lens to the entire lens, which leads to loss of vision. Certain types of opacities usually imply an inherited origin, and that animal should not be bred. Cataracts can be removed surgically with a good prognosis for the recovery of vision.
Generalized retinal atrophy	This is a disease of the visual cells in the retina. It starts at the edges, then to involve the whole retina. Night vision is lost first, then day vision.

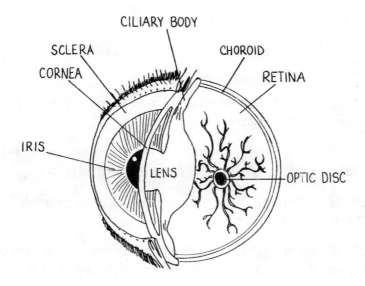

Diagram of the canine eye

Most owners notice that the dog's pupils are dilated, and he is not seeing well. Progressive Retinal Atrophy (PRA), a related disease, can start between two and five years of age. It is an inherited condition, and an affected animal should not be bred.

Retinal dysplasia

This is an abnormal development of the retina at birth. It can usually be diagnosed as early as eight weeks of age. It is seen in several forms that range from mild to disastrous. Samoyeds can suffer from a severe form of retinal dysplasia that is also seen in Labrador retrievers. It causes severe visual impairment and is associated with skeletal abnormalities. You should consult your veterinarian regarding the severity of the condition and how it will affect your breeding program.

References

ACVO Genetics Committee, 1995 and/or Data from *CERF All-Breeds Report, 1991-1995.*

Crispin SM, Barnett KC: "Dystrophy, degeneration and infiltration of the canine cornea." *J. Small AnimPract* 24:63, 1983.

Bussanich MN, et al: "Granulomatous panuveitis and dermal depigmentation in dogs." *J Am Anim Hosp Assoc* 18:131, 1982.

Halliwell, REW: "Autoimmune diseases in domestic animals." *J Am Vet Med Assoc* 181:1088, 1982.

Ekesten B, Narfstrom K: "Correlation of morphologic features of the iridocomeal angle to intraocular pressure in Samoyeds." *Am J Vet Res* 52:1875, 1991.

Ekesten B, Narfstrom K: "Age-related changes in intraocular pressure and iridocorneal angle in Samoyeds." *Prog Vet Comp Ophthal* 2:37, 1992.

Ekesten B, "Correlation of intraocular distances to the iridocorneal angle in Samoyeds with special reference to angle-closure glaucoma." *Prog Vet Comp Ophthal* 3:67, 1993.

Dice PF: "Progressive retinal atrophy in the Samoyed." *Mod Vet Pract* 1:59, 1980.

Meyers VN, et al: "Short-limbed dwarfism and ocular defects in the Samoyed dog." *J Am Vet Med Assoc* 183:975, 1983.

Acland GM, Aguirre GD: "Retinal dysplasia in the Samoyed dog is the heterozygous phenotype of the gene (*drd*) for short-limbed dwarfism and ocular defects." *Trans Amer College Vet Ophthalmol* 22:44, 1991.

M. K. Herrmann DVM, Diplomat ACVO, Gulf Coast Animal Eye Clinic, 1551 Campbell Road, Houston, Texas 77055, Graduate of Texas A&M 1970. Intern and resident Animal Medical Center New York, New York 1970-1973; Clinician Colorado State University 1973-1974; Board Certified in Veterinary Ophthalmology 1976

A Perfectly Photogenic Specimen

Since Bill's blue chair is a favorite of the Sams—two or three may lounge on it at a time—a clean sheet (with a rubber sheet underneath) are spread over it at all times. Remington, however, always rolls up this protective cover and pushes it aside. Perhaps he thinks that he is more photogenic against the blue upholstery.

Ch. Starshine's Remington O'Pixie (about 2½ years old)
Photo by Gay Glazbrook

Chapter 18

Skeletal Dysplasia

[The following chapter is abstracted mostly from monographs and other publications from the Orthopedic Foundation for Animals, Inc., with the kind permission of the Executive Director, Dr. G. G. Keller.]

Canine Hip Dysplasia

Hip dysplasia occurs in humans and most domestic animals. It is the most common cause of degenerative arthritis in most breeds of dogs.

Canine Hip Dysplasia (CHD) is a developmental disease caused by inherited multiple gene pairs. It is not a simple Mandelian heredity. Puppies may appear normal, but often show x-ray signs of deformity of the hip, which may become evident over a period than can be from several months to several years. By the age of two, 95% of dogs affected will show evidence of this condition on x-rays.

Because it is so important to recognizing this often-hidden trait, serious breeders are beginning to have their dogs x-rayed routinely, as a diagnostic measure. The Orthopedic Foundation for Animals (OFA) has become the unofficial national clearinghouse for x-ray interpretation and the analysis and compilation of data for veterinary medicine. To date the OFA has evaluated the hip x-rays of over 10,000 Samoyeds.[1]

Table I

Incidence of Canine Hip Dysplasia in selected breeds seen at OFA, 1974-1998 in descending order of incidence. Adapted from Hip Registry, OFA, 1998, with permission.[2]

Bulldog	71.4%
St. Bernard	47.1%
Bloodhound	25.9%
Chow Chow	21.5%
Old English Sheepdog	20.7%
German Shepherd	19.9%
Pit Bull	17.9%
Akita	14.6%
Alaskan Malamute	12.4%
Border Collie	12.4%
Samoyed	**11.9%**
Rhodesian Ridgeback	6.8%
Collie	3.0%
Siberian Husky	2.2%

The frequency of CHD is unknown since so few dogs are x-rayed. Most dogs are not registered with the American Kennel Club (AKC), and only 1.6% of those registered have had a hip evaluation.[3] Also, because many animals have obvious abnormalities, local veterinarians feel no need for consultation.

Heritability indices have been developed, which presumably measure how much of the variation in an animal's physical make up (phenotype) is genetic. A scale of 0 to 100% is used determine variations depending on the genetic background. A population of Samoyeds has been reported at 80%, while German Shepherds are reported at 40-50%. This data suggests that Samoyeds will respond very well to careful selection in breeding.

Behavior indicating possible CHD includes poor exercise tolerance, limping, early morning stiffness, slowness getting up and down, and awkward gait and stance. CHD is an inherited condition, and no physical variants cause or relieve it; however, excessive weight gain may reveal or worsen a latent CHD.

The anatomical mechanism of CHD is a shallow hip socket (acetabulum) and a looseness of the ligaments around the joint. Instability of the joint results in secondary degenerative changes (arthritis). The looseness around the hip joint (which consists of the acetabulum and the head of the femur—it is a ball-and-socket joint) can be tested through both physical and x-ray examination. When x-rays are done, the dog is given a short-acting anesthetic. Then a wedge-shaped pillow is placed between the dog's thighs, separating them with a bit of pressure. This makes it easier to see abnormalities on the film. An index has been devised in an attempt to quantify the looseness of the hip joint; however, it has failed to predict disease reliably.

Evidence of joint looseness on the x-ray is considered a significant finding, because loose joints are more prone to CHD. This laxity varies from breed to breed, as does hip joint anatomy. Therefore, evaluating what is normal must be done with the specific breed in mind.

Even normal canine hips are not perfectly symmetrical. Usually one hip socket is shallower than the other. Evaluations of hip dysplasia are based on the measurement of the side that is more shallow. Different breeds show varying degrees of skeletal maturity at birth. Samoyeds are known to be active and playing at a few weeks of age, and probably display early bone development on x-ray. Thus some breeds are fairly reliable in being evaluated when immature. Others, such as German Shepherds, Chows, and Border Collies must wait until they are two years of age (the standard) before x-ray evaluation can be considered accurate. See Table II.

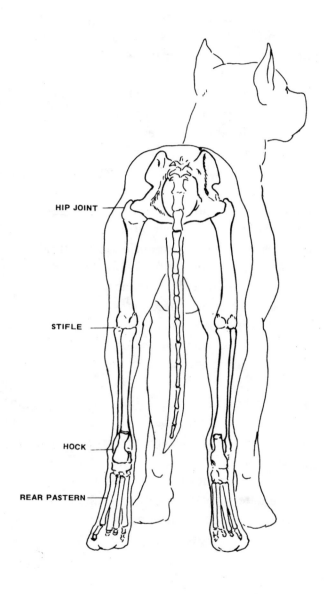

HIP JOINT

STIFLE

HOCK

REAR PASTERN

Table II

Reliability of x-raying puppies (less than 2 years) for CHD. Selected breeds. Percent with category later changed at maturity. (Age 2 years) Adapted from Corley and Keller.[4]

	False Positive %	False Negative %
Samoyed	3.4%	4.5%
Chow Chow	.08%	16.8%
German Shepherd	1.6%	14.3%
Akita	1.7%	3.4%
Labrador Retriever	3.3%	6.4%
Rhodesian Ridgeback	5.3%	2.6%
Border Collie	3.6%	14.3%

The standard caution to wait for maturity at 2 years before x-ray evaluation for CHD does not always apply. Some breeds may be evaluated somewhat earlier, allowing decisions with a fair degree of reliability. Note, however, that Border Collies, German Shepherds, Chows and some others have a sufficiently large degree of false negative results that "preliminary" x-ray testing of young animals is not advocated.

The OFA is a non-profit organization founded in 1966. It has the largest file of CHD data in the world. Their expert radiologists interpret hip conformation on x-rays sent to them, and the OFA compiles the data. Other diseases affecting the elbows, stifles, and back are also studied. The results of radiologist's evaluation are sent to the owner's veterinarian. The charge is currently $25.

Knowledgeable breeders require an OFA certificate of normal before they will use an animal in their breeding program.

The owner completes an OFA application form with appropriate information, including any tattoo, microchip, or DNA data.

During the estrus period, some bitches may undergo a "softening" of ligaments. A similar effect occurs with pregnancy and lactation. Thus, x-raying should be postponed 3 to 4 weeks before and after a heat period and after weaning.

Inactivity from altered health, management by owners, or climatic conditions reduces muscle tone in either sex. Evaluation may therefore be inaccurate and should be avoided in these circumstances, until healthy conditions return.

Evaluations of hip joints by OFA radiologists fall into one of seven classes. Three grades are considered normal and three dysplastic. There is a borderline classification in the middle. These classes are identified from best to worst as excellent; good; fair; borderline; mild dysplasia; moderate dysplasia; and severe dysplasia.

Some studies indicate that the incidence of hip dysplasia can be reduced. However, the number of dysplastic dogs may be incorrect, because so few dogs are x-rayed, as mentioned earlier. To detect a statistical decrease in a bad trait, scientists look for an increase in the opposite (good) trait, because it is the best indicator. Veterinarians have studied the percentage of dogs graded excellent by the OFA as an indication of improvement in the incidence of dysplasia over time. Table III displays data from the OFA which compares information gathered at two different time periods. This shows both "excellent" and dysplasia percentages for selected breeds, with a final column of the percent of evident reduction in dysplasia.

The number in the "excellent" category tended to increase across all breeds, while the number of dysplastics tended to decrease. These results are statistically significant.

Table III

Comparisons between time periods showing trend toward improvement in canine hips, presumable from careful breeding. Selected Breeds.[5]

Breed	Born Between 1972-1980		Born Between 1994-1995		% Decrease in Dysplasia
	% Excellent	% Dysplasia	% Excellent	% Dysplasia	
St. Bernard	4.5	47.8	0.9	39.5	17.4
Bloodhound	.05	25.9	1.8	17.5	32.4
Chow Chow	4.2	22.8	10.6	13.2	42.1
Old English Sheep	7.4	23.6	14.9	9.9	58.1
German Shepherd	2.5	20.7	3.3	16.9	18.4
Akita	7.5	17.5	21.5	9.3	46.9
Alaskan Malamute	10.4	14.1	17.6	7.0	50.4
Labrador Retriever	10.4	14.5	16.6	11.7	19.3
Samoyed	8.1	13.8	10.8	9.6	30.4
Rhodesian Ridgeback	13.9	12.2	23.7	2.4	80.3
Great Pyrenees	8.8	9.9	14.5	9.1	8.1
Siberian Husky	24.2	2.7	34.4	1.2	55.6

*Adapted from data of pamphlet: Hip Registry, OFA, with permission.[6]

Note the concomitant increase in the number of "excellent" gradings, along with the decrease in incidence of dysplastic identifications. Even the Siberian Husky, with very good hip phenotype showed improvement in both categories, with a substantial percentage change. Samoyeds showed a similar moderate improvement over time.

Interestingly, 40% of all registered Rottweilers were so examined in the 1989-1992 period. This may be significant in that a higher screening rate indicates greater owner interest and more careful breeding selection.

A sex difference was also noted in all breeds. Males showed a 51% overall increase in "excellent" rating, while only 27% of bitches showed this. The effects of estrus, whelping, and lactation on joint looseness are possible explanations.

The Orthopedic Foundation for Animals has repeatedly stressed the following recommendations for selective breeding, which is the only way to control hip dysplasia:

- Breed only normal dogs to normal dogs.

- The normal dogs should come from normal parents and grand-parents.

- The normal dogs should have greater than 75% normal siblings.

- Choose a normal sire that has a record of producing normal progeny.

- Choose replacement animals that have better hip joint conformation than their parents.

Neither championships nor a collection of trophies and ribbons are an index to genetic health and breeding desirability. Skeletal abnormalities may be present but detectible only through an x-ray examination. Pedigrees, littermates, and established progeny are more reliable indicators.

There is a perpetual need for education regarding hip dysplasia and the importance of selective breeding, since most dog fanciers will oversee breeding only for the few years that a specific bitch is fertile.

Veterinarians are hopeful that by identifying the specific genes involved and doing mass screening via DNA that faster improvement can be effected in the future.

End Notes

1   The Orthopedic Foundation for Animals, Inc. 2300 E. Nifong Blvd., Columbia, MO 65201-3856. (573) 442-0418.

2   Hip Registry; OFA

3   Kaneene, J. B. et al. "Retrospective Cohort Study of Changes in Hip Joint Phenotype of Dogs in the United States." *JAVMA*. Vol. 211, No. 12, Dec. 15, 1997, pp. 1442-1544.

4   Corley, E. A., & Keller, G. G. *Hip Dysplasia, A Guide for Dog Breeders and Owners*. Second Edition. OFA, 1989.

5   Dr. U. V. Mostosky, Personal Communication

6   Hip Registry; OFA

No Hip Problems Here!

Ch. Starshine's Remington O'Pixie dislikes loud noises. When the television volume was turned to extra loud one day, he eased close to the screen and lifted his leg. A sharp "Hey!" stopped him in mid air. "He's a critic," said Bill.

Ch. Starshine's Adoraduk O'Fanya

Photo by Pat Goodrich

Chapter 19

Canine Bloat

anine bloat is called Gastric Dilatation Volvulus Syndrome (GVD) by veterinarians. When it occurs, it constitutes an acute surgical emergency. The stomach is usually distended with air, markedly enlarged, and accompanied by a twisting upon itself (torsion or volvulus.)

Mortality from this condition is about 30 percent; however, if the illness is recognized early and treated promptly, the survival rate is about 80 percent. The dog will refuse food and attempt to vomit; his abdomen will be distended, and he will become lethargic. Sometimes chronic episodes of mild, recurrent vomiting, belching, and passing gas precede the acute event.

The condition is more prevalent in certain breeds (see Table I), and runs in the family of certain bloodlines. It is more likely in older, underweight dogs who gobble their daily meal of dry, processed dog food, and are of a nervous and fearful temperament. Conversely, a dog who feeds on moist food and table scraps and has a happy, easy going disposition will have a low incidence of bloat. No single event can be isolated as a triggering mechanism. Veterinarians recommend against exercise shortly after eating.

The incidence of cases seen at U. S. veterinary teaching hospitals has increased dramatically in the past thirty years. The cause of this escalation is not fully understood. Research studies are already underway.

Probably the most significant investigations have studied abdominal and chest anatomy. A study by Glickman et al. that compared animal sizes, as well as lower chest widths and depths, found a direct relationship between GDV, large size, and deep chests. Hall et. al., who studied surgical findings, found that longer ligaments at the gastric attachments in the abdomen allowed more gastric mobility and twistablility in dogs who had rotated stomachs. This significance is further emphasized by the fact that the volvulus recurred almost 100 percent of the time in dogs who had surgery but not gastropexy (attaching the stomach to the abdominal wall), while only 5 percent of dogs had a recurrence after gastropexy.

Prophylactic surgical repair has been suggested for dogs at high risk for GVD. Other preventive measures include diet modification; avoiding exercise near mealtime; giving the dog multiple meals or feeding him slowly, by hand; or slowing the dog's eating by putting rocks in the dish, or feeding him from a muffin pan.

In the January 1997 issue of *Bloat Notes*, Dr. Larry Glickman gives the following advice to dog owners: "If your dog suddenly develops a distended abdomen, appears uncomfortable, and gets progressively worse, rush the dog to a veterinarian, preferably one equipped to do emergency surgery. Gastric distension is a life-threatening condition, *even if the stomach is not rotated.* Immediate decompression is required to relieve pressure on blood vessels and to restore circulation to the heart, because shock can occur within minutes of the first clinical signs. Fluid therapy is indicated to treat shock, and drugs may be needed if the heart rhythm is irregular. This should be followed as *soon as possible* by surgery to reposition and immobilize the stomach (gastropexy) before it is irreversibly damaged. The best indicators of how well the dog will do post-operatively are its physical condition (state of shock) prior to surgery and the appearance of the stomach during surgery (since dead or dying stomach tissue implies a very poor prognosis). Intensive monitoring is usually required for several days postoperatively in case complications occur."

"If you suspect your dog has bloat, but the veterinarian dismisses it as a minor problem, inquire about radiographs [x-rays] to rule out GDV. If dilatation with or without volvulus is diagnosed and the stomach is decompressed, either by passing a stomach tube or by piercing the stomach with a large needle (trochar) passed through the body wall, the dog should be considered as a candidate for *immediate* surgery, unless its condition is too unstable to tolerate anesthesia. If the veterinarian recommends that surgery be delayed for any other reason, seek a second opinion immediately. Delay in surgery will increase the chance of the stomach rotating if it hasn't already, or will decrease the chance of the dog surviving if rotation has occurred."

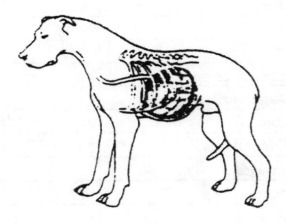

This illustration is reproduced from the masthead of Bloat Notes. *Note the dog's sagging ears and head, lowered tail, and abdomen bulging below the ribs.*

Table IV

Risk of Canine Bloat (Gastric Dilation-Volvulus Syndrome [GDV]). Various Breeds. In order of descending risk. Probabilities, with mixed breeds arbitrarily assigned a unit of one.*

Breed	Relative Risk Probabilities
Great Dane	41.4
Bloodhound	25.6
St. Bernard	21.8
Akita	16.4
Standard Poodle	8.8
Old English Sheepdog	4.8
German Shepherd	4.2
Alaskan Malamute	4.1
Collie	2.8
Labrador Retriever	2.0
Samoyed	1.6
Golden Retriever	1.2
Rottweiler	1.1
Mixed Breed	1.0
Cocker Spaniel	.06

Note that large and deep-chested pure breeds are much more predisposed to bloat. Samoyeds are not unduly at risk.

Indigestion? Never!

Cheryl Wagner's dog, Ch. Montego's Lady in White, DD, could polish off an ear of corn just like a person. She would hold it with a paw at each end, snap off the kernels from left to right, then repeat. As she ate, she turned the ear with her paws, continuing to gnaw across it until all was gone.

Mrs. Mason's Samoyed enjoying ice cream at the bar.

Courtesy of Sandra Flettner

Bibliography

The Alaskan Champion Sled Dog and Racing Association. *The Alaskan Champion Dog Musher*. Souvenir annual, 1952.

Baynes, Ernest Harold. *Polaris: The Story of an Eskimo Dog*. The MacMillan Co., 1931.

Behan, John. *Dogs of War*. New York: Scribner's, 1946.

Brearly, Joan McDonald. *This Is the Samoyed*. New Jersey: T.F.H. Publications, 1975.

Cohen, Stan. *The Forgotten War: A Pictorial History of World War II in Alaska and Northwestern Canada*. Missoula, MT, 1981.

Conn, Stetson, et al. "Guarding the United States and Its Outposts," in the *U.S.A. World War II Series*. Washington, D.C., 1954.

Dog World Annual, 1912, 1954.

Dog World Annual. Our Dogs (supplement). Great Britain, 14 December 1923, 14 December 1928, 5 December 1930, 16 December 1932, 14 December 1934, 13 December 1935, 10 December 1937, 1954, 1965.

Downey, Fairfax. *Dogs For Defense: American Dogs in the Second World War, 1941-1945*. Dogs for Defense, Inc., 1955.

Encyclopaedia Brittanica. The Encyclopaedia Co., Ltd., 1936.

Frank, Jay. "Corps K-9." *Army Life*, November 1942.

Frost, Denzil R. *A Centralized Source of Information for the Military Working Dog Program.* Typescript. 1990.

Garfield, Brian. *The Thousand-Mile War in Alaska and the Aleutians.* Garden City, NY: Doubleday, 1969.

Going, Clayton G. *Dogs at War.* New York: The MacMillan Co., 1944.

Kaneene, J.B., et al. "Retrospective Cohort Study of Changes in Hip Joint Phenotype of Dogs in the United States." *Journal of the American Veterinary Medical Association*, Vol. 211, No. 12, December 1997.

Keller, Gary. The Orthopedic Foundation for Animals (monographs), 1989-1993.

Kelly, Arthur. *Battlefire! Combat Stories from World War II.* Lexington: University Press of Kentucky, 1997.

Lauzlarich, Jan. *Your Samoyed.* Fairfax, VA: Denlinger, 1977.

McIntosh, Allen K., and Coke L. Westbrook. *A Review of the Military Programs.* 1968.

Montaigne, Fen. "Nenets—Surviving On the Siberian Tundra." *National Geographic* vol. 193, no. 3 (March 1998).

Morgan, Murray C. *Bridge to Russia: Those Amazing Aleutians.* Dutton, NY: Dutton, 1947.

Nansen, Fridtjof. *Farthest North* (Vols.I and II). New York: Harper and Brothers, 1897.

———. *Through Siberia: The Land of the Future.* London: Ballentyne Press, 1914.

O'Brien, John S. *By Dog Sled for Byrd: 1600 Miles Across Antarctic Ice.* Chicago: Thomas S. Rockwell Co., 1931.

Olsen, Sandra L. "Beware of Dogs Facing West." *Archaeology* vol 53, no. 4 (July-August), 2000.

Puxley, W. Lavallin. *Samoyeds*. London: Williams and Norgate, Ltd., 1934. Reprinted: Donald R. Hoflin, Arvada, CO, 1979.

The Samoyed Association of Great Britain. *The Samoyed*. London, 1961.

United States Air Force Manual. *U.S.A.F. Sentry Dog Program*. 1967.

United States Army. *War Dogs Trained by U.S. Army, Action, and Battle Areas*. Press Release. 2 February 1943.

United States Department of the Army. *Logistics (General), Horses, Mules, and Working Dogs*. 1961.

United States War Department Technical Manual #10-396. *War Dogs*. 1943.

Weir, Lila M., Roberta Hoerning, and Marj.VanOrnum. *Samoyed Champion Pedigrees*. Olympia, WA: Bastion Press, 1977.

Wilson, Pearl M., Valerie E. P. Auckram. *The Samoyed (New Zealand)*. New Zealand: The Cliff Press Ltd., 1961.

Wilson, R.L., with Greg Martin. *Buffalo Bill's Wild West: An American Legend*. New York: Random House, 1998.

Resources

Samoyed Club of America, Inc. Code of Ethics Guidelines

The constitution of the Samoyed Club of America, Inc. states that the club "Shall do all in its power to protect and advance the interests of the breed." In applying for and maintaining membership, applicants agree to further the club's objectives and conduct all their activities in connection with the breed in accordance with this Code of Ethics. A member of the SCA should conduct activities as follows:

Breeding — Each litter is the result of conscientious planning, including consideration of the parents' freedom from hereditary defects, type, soundness, temperament and general conformance to the official standard of the breed. The SCA member must be particularly concerned with the proper placement of puppies, both pet and show potential. The SCA member only breeds healthy, mature Samoyed adults, preferable 24 months of age, but at least 18 months of age. Prior to breeding any Samoyed, the SCA member obtains certification that its hips are normal from the Orthopedic Foundation for Animals, an equivalent foreign registry, or from a board approved radiologist and has its eyes certified free from genetically transmitted defects by a certified Veterinary Ophthalmologist. The SCA member knowingly breeds Samoyeds only to other registered Samoyeds.

Sales   The SCA member does not sell, consign, or transfer puppies or adults to pet shops, wholesale dealer, contest sponsors, or anyone who is known to degrade the Samoyed breed or purebred dogs, or to individuals contemplating breeding and/or sale to the aforementioned. The SCA member provides and requires written agreements signed by all parties prior to all transactions, sales, leases, and services and, accordingly, delivers all forms required for registration. The SCA member urges purchasers to spay or neuter any Samoyed who will not be shown in conformation, utilizing Limited Registration as appropriate. The SCA member does not actually transfer puppies to new homes until they are at least 7 weeks of age.

Health   The SCA member follows the guidelines of good kennel practice and provides all Samoyeds with maximum protection against communicable disease, consulting as necessary with a licensed veterinarian. The SCA member will not exhibit, release, or otherwise expose any Samoyed which is known to have been exposed to a communicable disease until the end of the incubation period for that disease.

Registration The SCA member accurately registers his Samoyeds with the American Kennel Club and abides by the AKC rules and regulations.

Exhibition The SCA member exhibits Samoyeds in conformation and obedience competition in conformity with the rules of the American Kennel Club and in the spirit of good sportsmanship. When traveling with Samoyeds, the SCA member takes reasonable precautions to maintain hotels and show grounds in a clean condition.

When confronted by a situation not covered by this Code of Ethics, the SCA member conducts himself or herself in the best interest of the breed and as he or she would like to be treated in similar circumstances.

Failure to conduct oneself in compliance with the Code of Ethics shall be considered prejudicial to the best interests of the Samoyed breed.

From 1999 S.C.A.'s "AT YOUR SERVICE"
Courtesy of the S.C.A.

Useful Addresses

The American Kennel Club
5580 Centerview Drive Suite 200
Raleigh, North Carolina 27606-3390

and 260 Madison Avenue
New York, New York 10016

A.K.C. Gazette
260 Madison Avenue
New York, New York 10016

Orthopedic Foundation For Animals
2300 Nifong Boulevard
Columbia, Missouri 65201

Canine Eye Registration Foundation
1248 Lynn Hall
Purdue University
West Lafayette, Indiana 47097

Responsible Pet Owners Alliance, Inc.
P O Box 701132
San Antonio, Texas 78270

Samoyed Club of America—Bulletin
681 Poor Boy Ranch Road
Wright City, Missouri 63390-2117

Samoyed Rescue of South Texas
11659 Jones Road PMB 103
Houston, Texas 77070
Website: www.samoyed.com\SRST.HTM

Noah's Ark Animal Sanctuary
11659 Jones Road PMB 103
Houston, Texas 77070
Website: www.noahs-ark-sanctuary.org

Owner Handler Association of America, Inc.
Rose Robischon
1100 Ridgebury Road
New Hampton, New York 10958